Companion to the Compendium of the Social Doctrine of the Church

Pádraig Corkery

VERITAS

In loving memory of my parents, John C. and Mary Corkery.

Their love and presence was always nourishing, affirming and enabling.

May they rest in peace.

First published 2007 by
Veritas Publications
7/8 Lower Abbey Street
Dublin 1
Ireland
Email publications@veritas.ie
Website www.veritas.ie

ISBN 978 1 85390 959 7

10 9 8 7 6 5 4 3 2

Printed in the Republic of Ireland by Betaprint Ltd, Dublin

Veritas books are printed on paper made from the
wood pulp of managed forests.
For every tree felled, at least one tree is planted,
thereby renewing natural resources.

Contents

Foreword

The Compendium of the Social Doctrine of the Church introduced by Cardinal Martino, President of the Pontifical Council for Justice and Peace, the body responsible for its production, stated that the social teaching of the Church is now made available to all – Catholics, other Christians, people of good will – who seek sure signs of truth in order to better promote the social good of persons and societies.

Catholic social teaching is a central and essential element of our faith. Its roots are in the Hebrew prophets who announced God's special love for the poor and called God's people to a covenant of love and justice. It is a teaching founded on the life and words of Jesus Christ, who came 'to bring glad tidings to the poor ... liberty to captives ... recovery of sight to the blind'(Lk 4:18-19), and who identified himself with 'the least of these', the hungry and the stranger (cf. Mt 25:45). The teaching and spreading of her social doctrine are part of the Church's evangelising mission (*Sollicitudo rei socialis,* John Paul II 1988).

True to this command, the Catholic Church in Ireland has a very proud record of involvement in the field of social concern. The various agencies and commissions of the Irish Bishops' Conference, the work of organisations such as St Vincent de Paul, Crosscare, the Legion of Mary and Conference of Religious of Ireland (CORI), and a host of parish and diocesan-based groups and agencies around the country provide a unique and very practical expression of the Church's commitment to the social, political and pastoral consequences of the Gospel.

Reverend Dr Pádraig Corkery, himself a former chairperson of the Irish Commission for Justice and Peace, has made an important contribution by making the social teaching of the Church more readily available to all, for study and reflection, through this work. He successfully builds a bridge between the wide-ranging text of the *Compendium* and its practical application to the many and varied social issues which are of concern today.

In it, he seeks to open up the *Compendium* itself in a narrative format that will be accessible to readers approaching the subject for the first time. Starting with the question 'Why Social Teaching?', Dr Corkery takes us on a journey through the key elements of Catholic social teaching, including the basic tools of evaluation and analysis and their application in the economic, political and ever more globalised world. All the defining terms are addressed here: the common good, the principles of subsidiarity and solidarity, the importance of participation and the universal destination of the goods of the world. A final chapter looks at the particular issues that Catholic social teaching addresses in the Irish context. Focusing on the recent pastoral letter of the Irish Bishops, *Prosperity with a Purpose* (Veritas, 1999) this *Companion to the Compendium of Social Doctrine of the Church* stands as a practical and important step towards meeting those social challenges from the perspective of Christian faith.

I welcome this publication and hope that it will be a well-read and studied text that results, not just in greater knowledge and understanding, but also and more importantly in a growth in action for justice and peace within a world that has great need for such commitment.

Raymond Field
Chairperson, Irish Commission for Justice and Social
Affairs (ICJSA)
A Commission of the Irish Bishops' Conference

Introduction

Over the past century and a half the Catholic tradition has developed a significant body of teaching in the area of Catholic social teaching or, as it has recently been called, Catholic Social Doctrine. This has been developed by the universal Church through the teaching of the popes in encyclical letters such as *Rerum Novarum* (Leo XIII) and *Centesimus annus* (John Paul II). The local Church across the globe has also issued a vast amount of teaching in this area. Examples from the local Church include those of the Irish Catholic Bishops (*Prosperity with a Purpose*) and the Catholic Bishops of England and Wales (*The Common Good*).

The fundamental insight of Catholic social teaching is that the Gospel invites us to engage and transform the world we live in. The essential Gospel demand – to love God and neighbour – must be acted on in the everyday world of politics, economics and social policy. Rather than making us indifferent to the world, Christian faith compels us to take responsibility for it. We are called to make Gospel values such as justice, respect for the dignity of each person and solidarity evident in the societies and world we inhabit. Catholic social teaching is quite clear that engagement with the world and concern for the plight of others is not an option for Christians but is at the very heart of what it means to be a disciple of the Gospel. In a memorable and often quoted phrase the Synod of Bishops in 1971 said that 'Action on behalf of justice and participation in the transformation of the world fully appears to us as a constitutive dimension of the preaching of the Gospel ...'.

Despite the priority given to social teaching in the life of the Church it appears to many that this dimension of the Christian life has made no great impact on the Christian family as a whole. Indeed, it is often said that Catholic social teaching is the Church's 'best kept secret'. While most Catholics and others are aware of Church teaching on sexuality and marriage they appear quite unaware of the Church's stance on issues in the social sphere. There are many reasons that could explain this phenomenon: the sheer volume and variety of the Church's social teaching; the low priority given to social teaching in Sunday homilies; the fact that some believers see issues of justice and inclusion at the periphery rather than at the core of the Christian vocation.

The *Compendium of the Social Doctrine of the Church* is an effort at tackling this lack of awareness, among Catholics and others, of the importance of the social dimension of the Gospel. In a single volume it presents the teaching tradition of the Church in a comprehensive and systematic way. It outlines clearly why care for others, especially the poor and vulnerable, and for the social fabric of our societies is a Gospel imperative. It identifies the core principles of the social-teaching tradition and shows how these principles were applied, in different times and historical contexts, to the complex worlds of economics and politics.

It is important to emphasise that the *Compendium* does not replace or make redundant the corpus of Catholic social teaching. It should be seen, rather, as a valuable resource that makes that tradition more accessible to a wider audience. It may give some a 'taste' for the subject and lead them to delve into the original documents and experience their great energy and sense of purpose.

The purpose of this book is to help individuals and groups experience the *Compendium* as a resource that both informs and inspires. It aims to present the content of the *Compendium* in a way that is more accessible by presenting the various topics in a more focused and less technical way. It clearly identifies the relevant paragraph numbers in the *Compendium* so that the reader can, if they so desire, pursue the subject at greater length.

The structure I have chosen is one that struck me as systematic and, hopefully, helpful. It begins in Part 1 by asking the *why* question. Why should the Christian community or individual be concerned with issues in the spheres of economics or politics? What is the Church's self-understanding that compels it to engage the structures of society rather than limiting its activities to the 'purely spiritual', the realm of the sacristy?

The Christian tradition has a unique way of looking at and understanding reality. It works out of a particular 'world-view' that has two central claims at its foundation. The first foundational claim is that the world we live in is a gracious gift from a loving God. The tradition also claims that this world has a purpose and a destiny. This is a very different starting point to that proposed by those who argue that the world is the result of chance and has no intrinsic meaning or destiny. Both world-views profoundly influence the priorities and values we pursue and the actions we perform. The second foundation on which the Christian world-view is constructed is that of the human person. The Christian tradition makes a very bold or radical claim about the human person that has immediate implications for how we react to and care for ourselves and others. This claim is that all persons are created 'in the image of God'. These foundational claims provide us with a way of understanding ourselves, others and the world we inhabit. They give us the 'eyes' through which we see reality. These foundational claims are clarified and unpacked in Part 2.

The central and core principles of Catholic social teaching are explored in Part 3. These principles were identified and sharpened over the decades as the Church grappled with a range of issues in the social sphere. Today they provide individuals and groups with ready tools that can be used to critique particular situations and to construct alternatives that are more in keeping with the values of the Gospel.

The application of the core principles of Catholic social teaching to issues in society is dealt with in Part 4. In particular the worlds of economics and politics and the reality of global conflict are evaluated from the perspective of these principles. The application of universal principles to the complex world of economics and politics can be a difficult task. It involves a prudential judgement that allows for the possibility of disagreement. People of good faith working out of the same tradition may disagree in their prudential judgements as to how universal principles and values are best promoted. Though all may be united in their commitment to the common good there may be legitimate moral pluralism as to how the common good is best promoted.

The final part of this *Companion* examines Irish society in light of the Church's social doctrine and the teaching of the Irish Catholic Bishops' Conference. Issues of justice, human rights and inclusion are not just issues that affect other societies. Justice issues are never simply 'over there'. The Church's social doctrine must be applied as vigorously to the local scene as it is applied to the global economy and to the lives of other communities.

In the past decade Irish society has experienced extraordinary change and development as it enjoyed the fruits of the Celtic Tiger. Its new-found wealth and energy brings with it considerable opportunities and challenges. The Irish Bishops identified as a key challenge the creation of a society that is more inclusive, just and compassionate.

I hope that this *Companion* will encourage and enable individuals and groups to discover the richness of the Church's social doctrine as it has developed over the centuries. The tradition has attempted in a disciplined way to bring the letter and spirit of the Gospel to bear on the societies and structures we inhabit. It is driven by the conviction that we are all responsible for the lives and well-being of our brothers and sisters across the globe. Having discovered the richness of the social doctrine tradition, I hope that readers will be inspired to work together to transform our world so that it better reflects the values of the Gospel.

PART 1

Why Social Teaching?

Chapter One

Why social teaching?

The Church's self-understanding

(*Compendium* Chapters 1, 2, 12)

Since the publication of *Rerum Novarum* in 1891 the Catholic Church has consistently and explicitly addressed issues of social justice. This has been done both at a global and local level. The *Compendium of the Social Doctrine of the Church* brings together in a systematic way the central insights and developments in the tradition of Catholic social teaching.

Some may ask why this is so? Should the Church not leave questions pertaining to justice, economic systems and human rights to politicians and governments? Should the Church concern itself only with prayer and worship?

The Church's involvement in social action and teaching flows from its self-understanding as a community centred on the person of Christ and the call of the Gospel to 'do likewise'. The Christ of the Gospels was concerned for the welfare of those he met and he encouraged his disciples to imitate his ways. In his lifestyle and preaching he highlighted values such as justice, respect for people, solidarity and peace. He constantly emphasised that love of God and love of our brothers and sisters are linked. For the Christian community the promotion and defence of the human person is a sign of its fidelity to the person of Christ and the Gospel vision.

In a more theological way the Christian community understands itself as a community called to Christian *orthodoxy* and *orthopraxis*; right belief *and* right living. This is succinctly summed up in the Gospel call to

Mt 25:34-6

Come you whom my Father has blessed, take for your heritage the kingdom prepared for you since the foundation of the world. For I was hungry and you gave me food; I was thirsty and you gave me drink; I was a stranger and you made me welcome; naked and you clothed me, sick and you visited me. In prison and you came to see me.

love of God and love of neighbour. This consistent Gospel call has lead to a strong rejection of a dualism that would reduce love of God to acts of worship only; that would in a sense leave the Gospel 'in the sanctuary'. Consistently over the centuries the Christian community has taught that our response to the invitation of Christ is to be seen in our attitudes and actions towards our fellow human beings. Furthermore, as disciples of Christ we are called to contribute to the building up of God's kingdom by bringing the spirit and values of the Gospel into daily life. As disciples we are both challenged and enabled to let the spirit and values of the Gospel shape our personal lives and the structures of our communities and societies. We are a 'new creation' (41–4) called and enabled to renew relationships with others and called to love our neighbour as ourselves 'because we are really responsible for everyone' (43). In the words of the Gospel we are called to be 'the salt of the earth and the light of the world', challenged to transform our lives and communities so that they more adequately reflect the ways of God (53).

The commitment of the Catholic tradition to issues of social justice and human well-being flows readily then from our understanding of the Gospel and the person of Christ. The Gospel challenges us not to be indifferent or hostile to the world we inhabit but to take it seriously and to take responsibility for it. As women and men of faith, who strive to shape our lives around the Gospel, our presence in the world is meant to be a dynamic, engaging presence that contributes to the transformation of the world (55).

A broken world

Our everyday experiences tell us that the world we inhabit is a very broken and uneven world. Human happiness and human pain and misery live side by side. As Christians how do we understand such negative realities as war, human cruelty and indifference, the deaths of millions through starvation in a world of plenty? How can they be squared with belief in a loving God and the 'good news' of the Gospel?

An important part of the Christian understanding of the world is a realism about human sinfulness. Christians are not naïve; they are not utopians. The biblical story of Adam and Eve gives us a good insight into the human condition. There is a tendency in all of humanity to wander from God's ways and become self-centred and unjust. The Gospel call is for a personal transformation so that we live more fully the values and spirit of the Gospel.

Furthermore the tradition of Catholic social teaching acknowledges that human sinfulness – greed, indifference, selfishness, hatred – can also become enshrined in the very structures and patterns of society. Consequently the tradition speaks about 'structures of sin' or 'social sin'. A good example of such a sinful structure would be the institution of apartheid where the sin of racial hatred and discrimination became enshrined in the laws and structures of a society.

However, as we know from the history of apartheid in South Africa, societies can be transformed. All societies have laws, customs and structures that reflect human choices and priorities. As such they can reflect both the best and worst of humanity; inclusiveness or exclusion, altruism or greed, concern or indifference. But societal structures and laws, since they are human constructs, can be changed for the better. Part of the Christian vocation is to engage the structures and laws of societies so that they better reflect the Gospel values of justice and respect for human dignity. Catholic social teaching has explicitly engaged in this ministry of critique and constructive proposal since the publication of *Rerum Novarum* in 1891.

Central insights of the Church's social doctrine

The central demand of Catholic social teaching is that the dignity of the human person be affirmed and promoted in our personal lives and in the economic, social and political spheres both domestically and internationally. In the Christian community the dignity of the human person is central. The Christian claim that we are created in the 'image of God' is a very radical claim with far-reaching consequences for how we view the human person. Christian anthropology – how we understand the human person – argues that each person has a dignity that is intrinsic and inalienable. This dignity flows readily from our reality as children of God. It also claims that we are more than one-dimensional; there is a 'Godly' or spiritual dimension to each person that needs to be acknowledged and affirmed. Indeed the Church understands itself as called to be a 'sign and defender of the transcendence of the human person' (49).

The person then is the measuring stick that the Catholic tradition of social teaching uses to evaluate and critique the economic, political and legal structures of society. Whatever attacks, diminishes or denies the dignity of the human person is of concern to Christians. Whatever negatively impacts on the human person and makes human flourishing more difficult is of concern to followers of the Gospel. Poverty, exploitation, injustice and violence all cause hurt and pain to the person and call for a response from believers. Through the virtue of solidarity the church 'stands with every man and woman of every time and place to bring them the good news of the

Kingdom of God' (60). It makes the Gospel present in the 'complex network of social relations' and strives to create communities that are more human because they are 'in greater conformity with the Kingdom of God' (63).

Social concern as optional?

Because of its self-understanding the Church is quite clear that the creation of societies that more adequately serve and promote the human person is 'an essential part of the Christian message ... This is not a marginal interest or activity, or one that is tacked on to the Church's mission, rather it is at the very heart of the Church's ministry of service' (67).

Because of this mission the Church has both a right and a duty to 'develop a social doctrine of her own and to influence society and societal structures' (69). A faith community gathered around the person of Christ and the Gospel 'cannot remain indifferent to social matters' (71) but must strive to transform them with Gospel values. The purpose of the Church's social doctrine is to guide 'peoples' behaviour' (73) so that their relationships respect the true nature of the human person and the purpose of creation as revealed through Revelation and reason.

Mt 22:34-40

Jesus said, 'You must love the Lord your God with all your heart, with all your soul, and with all your mind. This is the greatest and the first commandment. The second resembles it: You must love your neighbour as yourself. On these two commandments hang the whole Law and the Prophets too.'

Audience

Though the Church's doctrine has been developed out of a faith context it does not exclude the role of reason. A consistent claim of Catholic teaching is that the central features of morality can be grasped by human reason. In the Christian vision God did not abandon humanity but, rather, endowed us with reason that enables us to grasp the meaning and purpose of life. Through this appeal to reason Catholic social teaching has a 'universal applicability' (75) and appeal. This is seen clearly in the fact that the texts of the Church's social doctrine are addressed to 'men and women of goodwill' rather than simply to believers (84). The Church is firmly convinced that its social doctrines rooted in its understanding of the human person can be grasped by all who are sincerely looking for and open to the truth. For this reason too the Church engages in interdisciplinary dialogue with the human sciences and other branches of knowledge in her quest to create an ethos in society that is respectful of the human person (76–8).

The necessity of action

The Church by its very nature is called to proclaim the Gospel and to evangelise society. An essential part of this new evangelisation is a 'proclamation of the Church's social doctrine' (523). However, this proclamation must be accompanied by a firm commitment to action. Hence its social doctrine must be the reference point for its 'pastoral activity in the social field' (524). In today's world more than ever the Church's 'social message will gain credibility more immediately from the witness of action than as a result of its internal logic and consistency' (525). Indeed the Church must not only proclaim and work for conditions in society that enable human flourishing but must enshrine those same conditions in its own life.

Best-kept secret and hidden treasure

Within the life of the Church the corpus of social doctrine provides an 'extraordinary resource for formation ... especially true of lay-persons who have responsibilities in various fields of social and public life' (528). This resource could enable Christian lay-persons to be the yeast in society, bringing new life and inspiration into the world of work, politics and economics. However, experience indicates that 'this doctrinal patrimony is neither taught nor known sufficiently, which is part of the reason for its failure to be suitably reflected in concrete action' (528). In light of this reality the *Compendium* recommends that 'the formative value of the Church's social doctrine should receive more attention in catechesis' (529). The purpose of this exposure to the richness of the Church's social doctrine is to motivate action that will lead to the 'humanisation of temporal realities' (530). For this reason too exposure to social doctrine should feature prominently in institutes of Catholic education (532) and in the formation of candidates for the priesthood (533).

Cooperation with others

Because of its concern for the human person and community the social doctrine of the Church enables dialogue with civil and political leaders who are also called to serve the human family. It also, of course, enables dialogue and cooperation with other religious leaders and communities (534–7).

The unique role of the lay faithful

Though all Christians are called to be active subjects in bearing witness to the Church's social doctrine, the role of the laity is both unique and indispensable. They are called to a 'Christian discipleship which is carried out precisely in the world' (541). They give witness to Christ through their efforts at transforming the world in light of Gospel values. Their primary challenge is to bring 'faith and life together' by integrating their faith into their everyday lives. For the Christian disciple there cannot be two parallel lives in their existence:

on the one hand, the so-called 'spiritual life', with its values and demands; and on the other, the so-called 'secular' life, that is, life in a family, at work, in social relationships, in the responsibilities of public life and in culture. (546)

Lk 6:46

Why do you call me 'Lord, Lord' and not do what I say?

Indeed the Second Vatican Council judged the 'separation of Christian faith and daily life as one of the most serious errors of our day' (554).

Decision making

In deciding what to do in the concrete situation believers are guided by the virtue of prudence – 'the virtue that makes it possible to discern the true good in every circumstance and to choose the right means for achieving it. Thanks to this virtue moral principles are applied correctly in particular cases' (547). The social doctrine of the Church suggests that three distinct stages be observed when deciding on concrete action: reflection and consultation, evaluation and decision.

Engaging culture and politics

Through their service of the Church's social doctrine the laity can provide a unique service to the human person and to culture. There is a great need today to engage and enliven culture with the values of the Gospel, especially those of respect for human dignity and justice. We can say then that the 'ethical dimension of culture' must be a priority in the social action of the laity (556). The Church's social doctrine insists that the criterion of the human person 'is the criterion for shedding light on and verifying every historical form of culture' (558). Whatever diminishes or crushes the human person must be exposed and condemned. The denial of the religious dimension of the person is one example of a historic expression of culture that leads ultimately to the destruction of society (559).

Political involvement is a worthy and demanding expression of the Christian commitment to the service of others. Politicians inspired by their Christian faith can work towards the achievement of the common good and the creation of societal structures that are 'more and more consistent with the dignity of the human person' (566). Though Church social doctrine accepts the autonomy of the State it understands that 'autonomy' in a very precise way. In particular it argues that the State cannot be autonomous or free of the demands of the moral law. The state is bound – like all persons – to act in a way that respects the demands of the moral law discovered through reason and confirmed in Christian Revelation. The innate dignity and natural rights of the human person place real limits on the activities of the State (571).

How significant or weighty is Catholic social doctrine?

Though the Church is clear that the call to engage and transform society is a 'constituent part of the Gospel' questions still arise as to the exact 'weight' of Catholic social teaching. Are believers obliged to respond to it in their private and professional lives? Does it demand the same attention and respect as Catholic moral teaching on other subjects? Should it have an impact on choices and priorities pursued at home and in the workplace?

The Church is very clear on this important question:

Insofar as it is part of the Church's moral teaching, the Church's social doctrine has the same dignity and authority as her moral teaching. It is authentic Magisterium, which obligates the faithful to adhere to it. (80)

However, a distinction must be made between the articulation of fundamental principles (e.g. the right to strike, the right to fairness and justice in society) and the application of those same principles to complex situations. Hence the 'doctrinal weight of the different teachings and the assent required are determined by the nature of the particular teachings, by their level of independence from contingent and variable elements, and by the frequency with which they are invoked' (80). Faithful believers are obliged to assent to the core principles of Catholic social doctrine but may disagree on how best these principles are served in a particular economic or political strategy. Though united in their commitment to the common good, believers may, for example, legitimately disagree on its content and achievement.

Static or dynamic?

The Christian family is a living and dynamic family called to live the Gospel in a changing world. Over the centuries in response to changing landscapes it has teased out ever more completely the demands of the Gospel. In the same way the social doctrine of the Church is not static or complete but is, rather, a dynamic entity that engages with new situations.

Because it is always attentive to the changing nature of society 'the Church's social doctrine is characterised by continuity and renewal' (85). It draws universal values and principles from its reasoned reflections on the reality of the human condition. These are clarified and confirmed in the message of the Gospel. In this way its foundational principles do 'not depend on the different cultures, ideologies or opinions; it is a constant teaching' (85). On the other hand, the Church's social doctrine is open to continuous renewal and development as it applies these same principles to new circumstances. In this sense it can be understood as a 'work site' where work is always in progress; 'perennial truth penetrates and permeates new circumstances, indicating new paths of justice and peace' (86).

Brief historical sketch of Catholic social doctrine

The history of the Church's social doctrine shows development and clarification over the centuries. This can be seen in the following brief historical sketch beginning with the publication of *Rerum Novarum* in 1891.

Though the Church community always showed an interest in justice issues in society, the publication of '*Rerum Novarum* marks the beginning of a new path' (87). The encyclical often appears under the English title 'The Condition of the Working Classes' or 'The Workers Charter'. These titles reveal clearly its focus.

This encyclical has inspired 'Christian activity in the social sphere' over the decades and has been a consistent point of reference for this activity (89). Subsequent social encyclicals 'can be seen as an updating, a deeper analysis and an expansion of the original nucleus of principles presented in *Rerum Novarum*' (90).

In this great encyclical Pope Leo XIII confronted the ills of his time: the plight of the industrial worker in the newly industrialised cities of Europe. He strongly defended the rights of the workers to conditions that were in harmony with their dignity as persons. He clearly rejected a philosophy that reduced the worker to a 'cog in the wheel'. In the course of the encyclical he established principles that were developed and clarified in later Church documents: private property as a natural but non-absolute right; the right to a just wage; the natural right to form unions; the right to strike; the dignity of the human person as the fundamental criterion for evaluating economic and labour policies.

Quadragesimo Anno in 1931 addressed a very different world; a world of economic depression where the ability of the capitalist system to serve the common good and the demands of justice was seriously questioned. Pope Pius XI advocated a new social order based on justice and charity. He advocated a 'third way' – different from rigid capitalism and socialism – which was called 'vocationalism'. It placed a heavy emphasis on solidarity and cooperation and promoted the principle of subsidiarity. This encyclical was widely studied in Ireland and had an impact on several aspects of Irish life including the make-up of the Seanad and the development of the cooperative movement.

Dignitatis humanae, one of the most keenly debated documents of the Second Vatican Council, established the right to religious freedom as a fundamental right in society that should be recognised and promoted by the State. This right flows from the nature of the human person and the nature of religious truth; the human person must be free to search for religious truth and to embrace that truth in freedom. This development brought to an end centuries of Church hostility to the recognition of such a right.

Pope Paul VI in *Populorum progressio* addressed the justice issues surrounding the 'developing nations'. The document works out of a broad canvas and takes a more global view of issues of justice and peace. Though many new nations had gained political independence from their colonial masters they were still economically dependent and underdeveloped. He called for a model of 'integral' development that would include the development of the whole person and the community. This encyclical also called for solidarity between the First World and the developing world. In a memorable phrase, Pope Paul noted the link between underdevelopment, injustice and conflict: 'Development is the new name for peace' (98). If we are serious about the promotion of peaceful co-existence we must make international justice and solidarity a priority.

The Pontifical Commission *Iustitia et Pax* was 'established in 1967 to stimulate the Catholic community to promote progress in needy regions and international social justice' (99). It marked a significant development in the mission of the Church to bring the values of the Gospel to bear on the economic, social and political structures of our time. The establishment of local 'Justice and Peace Groups' was a natural and necessary development of the original initiative.

Pope John Paul II's encyclical *Laborem exercens*, published in 1981, reflected on the significance of work for the human person. The letter often appears with the English title *The Priority of Labour over Capital*, which sums up a central insight of this weighty work. The human person is more important than economic systems, wealth or profit. Indeed the document goes further and argues that all such systems are there to serve the human person and community. Another important point made in this encyclical is that human labour has a value primarily because it is a human person that is doing the work. This 'subjective' dimension of human work cannot be neglected but must rather be highlighted (101).

The encyclical *Sollicitudo rei socialis* in 1988 returned to the theme of development. Pope John Paul II critically reflected on the failed development of the Third World and outlined his understanding of authentic human development (102). Such human development is concerned with the whole person and cannot be achieved by mere possessions. Consequently, he argued that models of development that are built on an inadequate understanding of the human person – excluding the transcendent – are doomed to failure. The oneness of humanity and the need for solidarity among peoples and nations is strongly emphasised. In a development of Pope Paul VI's memorable phrase, peace is presented as the fruit of such solidarity: '*opus solidaritatis pax.*'

The encyclical letter *Centesimus annus* was written at a time of great change in the world. The collapse of the Soviet Bloc had occurred and the encyclical's reflections on that momentous event were eagerly awaited. It argued that the collapse of the Soviet Bloc was in part a consequence of its faulty anthropology; in denying the God-dimension of humanity the whole system was built on a faulty foundation that was unsustainable. While Pope John Paul II showed appreciation for democracy and the free economy, his understanding of both is quite nuanced. Both the free market and democracy are only acceptable if they are exercised within the limits set by the moral law. Consequently both must respect the dignity of the human person and the demands of justice and solidarity.

This brief overview indicates that over the past one hundred years the Church in its social teaching has explicitly brought the light of the Gospel to bear on the social, economic and political structures of our world. It has identified central principles and values that are necessary for the flourishing of the individual and society. It has affirmed structures and practices that recognise and promote the dignity of the person. It has identified and condemned structures and attitudes that assault human dignity and promote injustice. It has proposed ways in which attitudes and structures can be transformed to better reflect and promote the dignity and oneness of the human family.

***

This first part of the *Companion* has outlined the reasons why the Christian family is concerned with social matters. It is an essential and undeniable consequence of the nature of the Church; a community of persons gathered around the person of Christ and responding to his call to 'do likewise'. This section also highlighted the decisive role of the laity as bearers of the social doctrine tradition. As Christian disciples they are called in a special way to engage and transform the structures of society so that they are in harmony with the values and insights of the Gospel.

Lk 6:31

Treat others as you would like them to treat you.

Part 2 will now look at some of the decisive features of the Christian world-view that have an impact on the formation and content of Catholic Social Doctrine. The Christian family looks at and understands the world in a unique way; it has a particular faith-stance that influences its actions and priorities. It has a particular way of understanding and valuing the gift of creation and the significance of the human person. These will now be explored in Part 2.

Pointers for further discussion

1 '[O]n the one hand, religion must not be restricted to "the purely private sphere", on the other, the Christian message must not be relegated to a purely other-worldly salvation incapable of shedding light on our earthly existence' (71).

- In your experience who understands religion as 'purely private' or as something to be shared in society?

- What might be the dangers for society if religion is understood as 'purely private'?

- What is the challenge for us Christians, called as we are to participate in society?

2 'Fostering a social and political culture inspired by the Gospel must be an area of particular importance for the lay faithful' (555).

- Discuss the phrase 'social and political culture inspired by the Gospel'. What does it mean?

- In the context of your own parish or community group explore concrete ways in which you could work to foster or build such a 'culture'.

- What are the Gospel values or insights that seem different to some of the values or ideas pursued in society today?

3 'This doctrinal patrimony [the Church's social doctrine] is neither taught nor known sufficiently, which is part of the reason for its failure to be suitably reflected in concrete behaviour' (528).

- Do you agree that Catholic Social Doctrine is 'neither taught nor known'? What has contributed to this situation?

- Do you think that the Church's teaching on social matters is difficult to communicate?

- Is there a concrete action that you can take, individually or as a group, to develop your understanding of Catholic Social Doctrine?

PART 2

Solid Foundations: The Christian World-view

The Christian family understands life through its faith in the central mysteries of creation, sin, incarnation, redemption and resurrection. In a very real way faith in these realities gives Christians the 'eyes' through which they see and understand themselves, others and the world they inhabit. How we understand the origin and destiny of humanity and the origin of the world we inhabit has a profound impact on what we value, respect and prioritise.

Jn 3:16

Yes, God loved the world so much that he gave his only Son, so that everyone who believes in him may not be lost but may have eternal life.

Christian faith gives us a world-view or a perspective on life that has an impact on decision making. People of other faiths also work out of a world-view that gives a direction and shape to their choices. People who deny the reality of God also work out of a context that influences their choices and decisions.

How we 'see' and understand ourselves and our world then gives Christians and others the context out of which they make reasoned decisions. The Christian world-view is built on the twin foundations of an understanding of the origin, meaning and purpose of the created world and an understanding of the nature, significance and destiny of the human person. On these foundations the Christian perspective on everyday realities – politics, ecology, economics, war – is constructed. Seeing the world as a gift from a gracious God fosters in us a sense of reverence, thanks and responsibility. Accepting that the world has a purpose encourages us to discover that purpose and to strive to live in harmony with it. The second foundation of the Christian vision proposes that every human person was created in the 'image of God'. This should lead us to act in ways that respect the sacredness and uniqueness of each person. It also alerts us to the transcendent dimension of humanity; we are not 'one dimensional' and the Godly dimension must be acknowledged and promoted if we are to respect the nature of the person. Equally the acceptance of Jesus as the model for humanity motivates us to 'do likewise'; to reflect the attitudes and actions of Jesus in our everyday encounters with people.

Chapter Two

Creation as a gift to all of humanity from a loving God

(Compendium Chapter 10)

In the biblical account of creation given in Genesis, Chapter 1, God both created the world in an act of love but also declared that it was 'good' (451). Furthermore God entrusted creation to humankind to care for it and to avail of its resources wisely. This vision of the origin of creation and of the role assigned to humankind underpins the Church's perspective on created reality. Humankind is challenged to use its God-given creativity and genius in a way that is beneficial to the human family while respecting the 'gift' of creation (456–60). We are to be responsible stewards availing wisely of the gifts bestowed on us. The vision of creation as 'gift' should generate a response, at the level of attitude and action, that includes a sense of thankfulness, awe and wonder.

Gen 1:1

In the beginning God created the heavens and the earth.

Ecological crisis

In recent decades there has been increasing emphasis at national and international level on the ecological crisis. There is a growing awareness that our relationship with the environment is destructive and unsustainable. Pollution and global warming are just two examples of the destructive impact of human activity on the environment. This crisis in the relationship between humankind and the environment (461–5) must be both acknowledged and analysed. It is necessary to ask why this relationship became so destructive and, ultimately, unsustainable.

The primary reason is that the environment was, for too long, seen only as a resource to be constantly exploited and manipulated. Humankind consistently worked out of an ethic of domination rather than an ethic of responsible stewardship. In this vision nature and the environment were to be dominated and were seen to have value only in terms of their usefulness to humanity. The intrinsic goodness and worth of creation as a gift from God was either denied or lost.

Besides being counter to the Christian vision, the attitude and practice of seeing nature only as a resource, and not 'home', was also built on erroneous presuppositions. It was accepted uncritically that there was an infinite quantity of energy and resources available to be harnessed for the needs and wants of humanity (462). Furthermore, it was believed that these could be renewed quickly and that the negative effects of the exploitation of nature could be easily absorbed. This unhealthy attitude to the created world was also encouraged by a consumerist ethic with its emphasis on having rather than being.

This destructive relationship to creation was also the fruit of an increasing loss of the sense of God in our world. The Christian stance links humankind and creation in the one act of a loving God. Both humankind and nature have their origin and purpose in God. If the reality of God is denied a destructive separation of humankind from creation can easily result (464).

From the perspective of the Christian vision of reality a correct understanding of the environment prevents the utilitarian reduction of nature to a mere object to be manipulated and exploited. It is rather a 'gift' that brings humankind many benefits and should be enjoyed with gratitude and reverence. This understanding also prevents the other extreme of absolutising nature and placing it 'above the dignity of the human person' (463).

Since the environment is a gift for all there is a shared responsibility on all to protect it (466). We have a special and urgent responsibility towards future generations so that they may experience the wonder and beauty of nature and benefit from its fruits. It is imperative therefore that economic programmes should respect the integrity and cycles of nature. A programme that is respectful of the environment 'will not have the maximisation of profits as its only objective' (470). It will look rather at the 'bigger picture' – the integrity of the natural order and the needs of future generations.

In recent years significant questions have been asked about new forms of biotechnology in several areas including agriculture, animal farming and medicine (472). The Christian vision, in principle, 'makes a positive judgement on the acceptability of human intervention in nature, which also includes other living beings, and at the same time makes a strong appeal for responsibility' (473). Developments in this area must be evaluated by their impact on living beings, the environment and the well-being of future generations. If they damage any of these they are morally unacceptable. Those working in the area of biotechnology must also keep in mind that the material they work on 'belongs to the patrimony of humanity and is destined also to future generations' (477). In this area of science there is a special need for information and transparency so that public debate can be informed and constructive. This should help avoid the two extremes of uncritical over-enthusiasm or unjustified alarmism (480).

With regard to the environmental crisis it is important to remember that it is connected to poverty 'by a complex and dramatic set of causes' (482). The reality is that 'hunger and poverty make it virtually impossible to avoid an intense and excessive exploitation of the environment' (482). Those who are hungry are often forced to adopt lifestyles and work practices that are destructive of the environment. An adequate response to the environmental crisis must therefore also address the reality of poverty and inequality. In this regard the principle of the universal destination of the world's goods – the fruits of the earth were meant for all – provides a fundamental moral principle.

Ultimately a response to the environment crisis demands both a change of attitude and 'the adoption of new lifestyles' (486). Our attitude should be one of gratitude and appreciation for the gift of creation in all its beauty and diversity. Consumer choices should be determined by reference to the common good of humanity rather than by a rugged individualism or a blind consumerism. Our sense of shared humanity should lead us to embrace lifestyles that respect our shared inheritance – the environment – and enable all to share of its fruits.

Pointers for further discussion

1 'The biblical vision inspires the behaviour of Christians in relation to their use of the earth, and also with regard to the advances of science and technology.' (456)

- From your knowledge of the Bible explore together your understanding of its vision for our 'use of the earth'.

- How do you think this vision connects with contemporary environmental challenges?

- Does the biblical version offer something unique to science and technology?

2 'Serious ecological problems call for an effective change of mentality leading to the adoption of new lifestyles ...

There is a need to break with the logic of mere consumption and promote forms of agricultural and industrial production that respect the order of creation and satisfy the basic human needs of all.' (486)

- What do you think this 'logic of mere consumption' actually means and how do you experience it in your daily life?

- Who are the people who need to change their lifestyle and what are the practical changes that could make a significant difference to our world?

- Is it enough for individuals to undergo a 'change of mentality'?

Chapter Three

The Human Person

(Compendium Chapters 3, 5, 6)

The Christian vision of life places the human person at the very centre and makes the human person the criterion by which we evaluate economic, political and social structures. The Christian claim that we are created in the 'image of God' is a very profound one. It claims that each one of us mirrors the majesty, sacredness and wonder of God. This understanding of the human person – Christian anthropology – has profound implications for how we understand ourselves and behave towards others. These implications will be teased out at the beginning of this chapter.

I. CHRISTIAN ANTHROPOLOGY

The central features of this Christian anthropology can be unpacked as follows:

1. A radical equality of persons

The Christian claim is that all persons are created in God's image. This claim extends not just to believers or to the virtuous but to all persons. The Christian story furthermore calls us to a care and love that is universal; that sees the 'image of God' in every person irrespective of their colour, ethnic origin, religion or sexual orientation.

2. The transcendent nature of the human person

Christian anthropology, with its claim that we 'image' God, presents the human person as a 'unified totality' comprising of body and soul. An adequate understanding of the human person recognises the transcendent or Godly dimension of humankind; we are more than one-dimensional. There is a spiritual dimension to the human person – the quest for God – that needs to be recognised and promoted in our engagements with people. The Christian understanding of life sees God as our origin and destiny. We come from God and we return to God. This understanding of the human person – that we are more than one-dimensional – provides a powerful critique of consumerism and materialism. There is a depth dimension to the human person – our relationship with the Creator God – that cannot be denied or satisfied by material comfort. Political, economic and social structures that deny this dimension of humanity fail to promote or serve the authentic needs of the human person and community. Indeed political systems that deny the transcendent nature of humanity are built on an inadequate foundation that inevitably leads to their collapse. The fate of the Soviet Bloc provides a clear example of such a collapse.

3. The intrinsic dignity of the human person

The Christian tradition claims that as persons we have a dignity that is intrinsic to us. Our dignity flows naturally from our reality as sons and daughters of God, created in God's image. Human dignity was further affirmed by the central event of the Incarnation: the reality that Christ entered human history and took on human form.

This approach to the human person and their dignity is very different from an approach that would make our dignity dependent on our achievements, virtue, social standing or health. This approach also rejects the notion that our dignity is conferred on us by the State or by our families. Rather it belongs to us because of who we are: children of God. The Christian vision calls us to recognise, protect and promote the dignity of each person in our personal actions and societal structures.

4. The human person as relational and social by nature

The human person is born of and into human relationships. We are by nature social, called into a web of human relationships that are essential for our flourishing as persons. The God of Christian Revelation is a God that exists as a community of persons – Father, Son and Holy Spirit – and provides a model for human relationships. The protection and promotion of the social nature of the person is essential if the common good of society is to blossom. The need for freedom in society to form human relationships is one direct implication of this understanding of the human person. This freedom extends to the whole gamut of relationships – intimate, friendship, cultural, sporting, political – that people form and which contribute to their flourishing and that of society.

5. The reality of sin

The Christian understanding of the human person is not naïve or utopian. Christian Revelation in the Book of Genesis introduces us to the Fall of our first parents, Adam and Eve. What is immediately obvious from the account is that the consequences of that first sin are all described in relational terms. The state of harmonious relationships in 'paradise' is now shattered and replaced by relationships that are fraught with difficulties. Adam and Eve hide from God and are ashamed. They turn on one another and squabble over who was responsible for their plight. The harmonious relationship between nature and Adam and Eve is also changed; they must now earn their living through the 'sweat of their brow'. The biblical story reminds us that we can all be sinful and wander from the demands of God's law and human dignity. Greed, hatred and selfishness can shape our attitudes and actions both at a personal and societal level. These distort the families and communities we belong to and make them less responsive to the human person created in God's image.

Catholic social doctrine also recognises that human sinfulness can become enshrined in the very fabric of society. The personal sin of greed or racial hated can become part of the economic, legal or political structures. In an analogous sense we can therefore talk of 'structures of sin' or 'social sin'. Apartheid is a clear example of a 'sinful structure' where the sin of racial discrimination became enshrined in the laws and customs of a society. These structures were maintained by the sinful attitudes and actions of individuals or, indeed, by their indifference to the plight of others. The language of 'structures of sin' does not, therefore, clear us of personal responsibility for the societies we inhabit.

However, Christian Revelation also indicates how this tendency in humanity can be transformed through faith in Christ and the following of the Gospel. Through God's grace and the inspiration of the Gospels we can live in 'right relationship' with God and our brothers and sisters. The challenge for Christians is to bring the light of the Gospel into our personal lives, relationships and communities. In this way the ethos of society can be transformed so that it more adequately responds to the demands of human dignity.

Christian anthropology and human rights

Catholic social teaching has, over the centuries, reflected on the implications of this Christian anthropology for society. It argues that the human person must be at the centre of all economic, social and political activity. This is the criterion by which these realities must be evaluated.

The systems of the world – economic, social and political – are there to affirm, serve and promote the human person and family. In his encyclical *Laborem exercens* Pope John Paul II made this point forcefully: the right to private property, economic policies and political systems are subordinate to the human person.

The identification and proclamation of human rights is seen by the Catholic tradition as one of the most significant steps on the journey towards the full recognition of the demands of human dignity. The Universal Declaration of Human Rights adopted by the United Nations in 1948 was praised by Pope John Paul II as a 'true milestone on the path of humanity's moral progress' (152).

Source and scope of rights

A Christian anthropology locates the ultimate source of human rights in the very nature of humankind created by God. It rejects approaches that find the source of human rights in the mere will of human beings, in the reality of the State or in public powers. We are not given human rights nor do we have to earn them; they are an intrinsic part of being human.

It further claims that these rights are 'universal, inviolable, inalienable' (153). *Universal* because they are present in all human beings, without exception of time, place or subject. *Inviolable* insofar as 'they are inherent in the human person and in human dignity' and because 'it would be vain to proclaim rights, if at the same time everything was not done to ensure the duty of respecting them by all people, everywhere, and for all people'. These rights are *inalienable* insofar as 'no one can legitimately deprive another person ... of these rights, since this would be to do violence to their nature'. This understanding of the source, nature and scope of human rights provides us with a powerful criterion with which to critique the actions of individuals and society. It also provides a vision or world-view that should inspire Christians, and people of good will, to promote and defend human rights across the globe.

Jas 2:1

Do not try to combine faith in Jesus Christ, our glorified Lord, with the making of distinctions between classes of people.

Thankfully the universal nature of human rights is readily acknowledged in our day. Indeed one could say that our time is particularly in tune with the language of human rights. It is a cause that has caught the imagination of citizens, media and political parties. Most societies and politicians see themselves as strong advocates of human rights and are always seeking new ways to expand these rights.

A list of rights

The affirmation of human rights as intrinsic to every person leaves us with a very practical question about the identification of rights. How many human rights are there? Is there a hierarchy of human rights? How can conflicting rights be reconciled? Are human rights absolute or can they be curtailed by, say, the common good of society? These are very important questions that have generated heated debate in many countries.

The reality of disagreement on these fundamental questions lay at the heart of the disagreement on the 'right to' abortion and euthanasia in society. The Church in its social teaching has attended to these questions in detail and with a sense of urgency. Pope

John Paul II in *Centesimus annus* set out a list of human rights which included: the right to life, the right to develop one's intelligence and freedom in seeking and knowing the truth, and the right freely to establish a family (155). The right to life, from conception to natural death, is recognised as the primary right that is the condition for the exercise of all other rights. The recognition and honouring of this right excludes the practises of abortion and euthanasia.

The right to religious freedom is another central right that must be recognised in society (155). This right was clearly and unambiguously affirmed in the Declaration on Religious Freedom of Vatican II. The human person has the duty and, hence, the right to seek the truth in matters religious and moral. However, this search for truth must be carried out in a way that is respectful of the human person and the nature of religion. For those reasons it can only be carried out in the context of freedom. No one should, therefore, be coerced or forced to act contrary to their beliefs in society. However, like all rights exercised in a community, the right to religious freedom has limits too. It must respect the rights of others and the common good of society. The importance of the right to religious freedom is highlighted by the fact that Pope John Paul II saw that right as providing the source and synthesis of all human rights. He understood religious freedom as 'the right to live in the truth of one's faith and in conformity with one's transcendent dignity as a person' (155).

Rights and duties

The Catholic tradition has long proclaimed that rights and duties go hand in hand, that they are 'indissolubly linked' (156). In exercising our rights we have an obligation to respect the rights of others and the common good of society. Equally there is a duty on others to acknowledge and respect our rights. This linking of rights and duties is in sharp contrast with a ruggedly individualistic approach to rights that fails to see the person as a person-in-community.

Rights of nations and peoples

The language of human rights has expanded in recent decades to include the rights of peoples and nations. Indeed we could say that the rights of nations are simply human rights fostered at the 'specific level of community life' (157). The rights of nations explicitly mentioned by the *Compendium* include: a fundamental right to existence, a right to its own language and culture and a right to shape its life according to its own traditions.

The abuse of rights

Reality, sadly, reveals that the bold proclamation of human rights is sharply contradicted by the reality of human rights violations. The reports of human rights agencies and the work of the media highlight, on a daily basis, the abuse of human persons. The realities of war, genocide, torture, deprivation, exploitation of workers, trafficking in human persons are well documented. In the words of the *Compendium* there is a gap between the 'letter' and the 'spirit' of human rights that needs to be challenged by the Church and other agencies dedicated to the common good of humanity (158–9).

Church: Defender of human rights

Because of her self-understanding the Church sees herself as called to proclaim and defend human rights. This witness must, firstly, be exercised in the life of the

Church. To be an authentic proclaimer of human rights it must first respect human rights within the Church community. It must live the demands of justice before it can credibly challenge others to do so. There is a need therefore for an ongoing examination of Church practices and lifestyles.

Secondly, she must both proclaim boldly the source and scope of human rights and energetically denounce any and every violation of these rights. This task can be shared with others of good will, including fellow Christians, other religions and government and non-government agencies (159).

The family

Given the social nature of the human person the Church in its social doctrine attaches special importance to the family and its role in society. The family is considered the first natural society which, like the person, has natural or 'underived' rights that must be respected (211). The family is the first and vital cell of society where the person experiences for the first time love and self-giving, becomes aware of their dignity and begins the journey towards development and maturity (212). In this way the family makes a unique and irreplaceable contribution to the good of society (213/14). As a natural institution the family exists prior to the State and the State exists to protect and promote it. In respecting the rights of the family the State should avail of the principle of subsidiarity which directs the State to help individuals and families while respecting individual responsibility and initiative. The importance of this principle will be clarified in Part 3, when we will examine the central principles of Catholic Social Doctrine.

In its duty to protect the family the State must give special attention to the institution of marriage (215–20). In the Christian understanding marriage is

Mt 19:4

Have you not read that the creator from the beginning made them male and female and that he said: This is why a man must leave father and mother, and cling to his wife, and the two become one body?

both a natural institution, flowing from our nature as persons called into relationships, and an institution willed by God. The characteristics of marriage, which are accessible to human reason, are totality, unity, indissolubility and fidelity. The State in its service of the common good should strive to create an ethos that is supportive of marriage and the family. This raises important questions concerning the content of the civil law on same-sex unions (228), reproductive technologies (235), cloning (236) and the education of children (238–43).

Pointers for further discussion

1 'A just society can become a reality only when it is based on the respect of the transcendent dignity of the human person. The person represents the ultimate end of society, by which it is ordered to the person.' (132)

   • How is the 'transcendent dignity of the human person' talked about in society today?

   • Can you identify groups or projects in our society that promote the inherent value of the human person?

   • How do we deny the value of the human person in our attitudes and practices in society?

   • How should we as Christians respond to this world-view?

2 'The movement towards the identification and proclamation of human rights is one of the most significant attempts to respond effectively to the inescapable demands of human dignity. The Church sees in these rights the extraordinary opportunity that our modern times offer, through the affirmation of these

rights, for more effectively recognising human dignity ...' (152)

- Discuss what you think the 'identification and proclamation of human rights' means in practical terms.

- Do you think people in society today have a clear understanding of the roots and importance of human rights and their relationship with duties?

- How might your group or parish promote human rights as a way of affirming the value of every human being?

II. THE SIGNIFICANCE OF WORK

(Compendium Chapter 6)

A cursory glance at the Christian scriptures reveals some fundamental truths about the nature and significance of human work. The biblical injunction to rest on the Sabbath (258) reveals something important about work and invites us to put work in perspective. Work, though important, ought never become an idol since God alone is our origin and destiny. Through Sabbath rest we have time to experience anew God's creation and to enjoy the company of loved ones. For believers, Sunday is, of course, a special time for prayer and for giving praise to God.

Mk 6:3

This is the carpenter, surely, the son of Mary, the brother of James and Joset ...

Because of this the Church in its social doctrine sees rest from work as a *right*. It argues that as God rested on the seventh day so too human persons, created in God's image, 'are to enjoy sufficient rest and free time that will allow them to tend to their family, cultural, social and religious life' (284). Furthermore the Church's doctrine argues that 'public authorities have the duty to ensure that, for reasons of economic productivity, citizens are not denied time for rest and divine worship' (286).

The Gospel narrative also reveals significant truths about work and its importance. In the first instance Jesus is portrayed as a man of work (259–63) who worked in the workshop of Joseph (Mt 13:55, Mk 6:3). For Christians the example of Christ, on all issues, is formative; it always challenges us to 'do likewise'. It is also noteworthy that in his parables he rebuked the useless servant and praised the prudent servant (Mt 24:46, 25:14-30). Jesus also reminds us not to be enslaved by work; that work is not an end in itself.

The New Testament writers confirm these truths about the value of work. They urged the new communities of believers to work hard and to share with others (264). They were, furthermore, to undertake their work in the style of Christ and make it an occasion for Christian witness, commanding the 'respect of outsiders' (1 Thes 4:12).

The insights of *Rerum Novarum*

The significance of work for the human person has been the subject of reflection by the Church over the centuries. In this regard the encyclical *Rerum Novarum*, in 1891, made a decisive and prophetic contribution (267–9). As already indicated in Part 1 the encyclical was written at a time of great unrest and agitation in Europe. With the spread of the Industrial Revolution society had changed from a predominantly agrarian society to an increasingly industrial one. Great numbers of peoples left the countryside to seek employment in the new industrial cities. The conditions the workers encountered were, by and large, very harsh and resulted in much human suffering. Workers experienced long working hours in dangerous working conditions and received inadequate pay. As a consequence unrest spread across the major cities as workers vented their anger. The appearance of the Communist movement with its denial of the right to private property added fuel to this volatile situation.

Pope Leo responded to this reality by reflecting on the plight of the workers in the encyclical *Rerum Novarum*, which is most often published in English with the title *The Workers Charter* or *On the Condition of the Working Classes*. As noted in Part 1 the title gives us a clear indication of its focus and content.

The encyclical offers a clear and robust defence of the intrinsic dignity and inalienable rights of the workers. The dignity of the worker must, he argued, be respected by employers and the market. The worker cannot be viewed as a mere 'cog in the wheel' nor should human labour be viewed just as a commodity to be bought and sold. The encyclical condemned the conditions and work practices of the day that reduced the worker to a state of 'slavery'. Pope Leo XIII argued that workers were entitled to a 'just wage' that enabled the worker and his family to live in a dignified manner. He rejected as inadequate the practice of the time – the 'agreed wage'– where wages were set solely by the market without reference to the human needs of the worker. Out of sheer necessity workers could 'agree' to work for wages that were inadequate for their needs and in conditions that denied their humanity. This distinction between the 'agreed wage' and the 'just wage' has been a consistent element of Catholic social doctrine since the time of Pope Leo. Recent teaching has applied it also to the trade agreements between the developed world and the developing world. Such agreements should honour the demands of justice – adequate remuneration for labour and raw material – rather than just the conditions of an 'agreed' contract.

The encyclical strongly argued that the right to form unions and to campaign for better working conditions was a natural right. Leo, of course, insisted that such unions and their campaigning should be peaceful. He further argued that unions should ensure that the spiritual dimension and needs of the human person be recognised and facilitated by employers. The recognition and encouragement of workers unions in the encyclical displeased many wealthy employers of the day. They had hoped that the Pope would condemn unions with the same vigour with which he rejected communism.

Laborem exercens

Pope John Paul II in his encyclical *Laborem exercens* has given the Church its most weighty and profound reflection on the nature and significance of work for the human person. This is clearly seen in the *Compendium*'s treatment of work; it is heavily dependent on the insights and distinctions made by John Paul II.

In *Laborem exercens* he strongly emphasises the subjective dimension of work; it is a person who does the work. Hence work has dignity, not because of the work done, but because it is a person who does the work. This subjective dimension takes precedence over the objective dimension. An implication of this approach is that work is not to be considered as simply a commodity or an impersonal element of the world of industry but rather as 'an essential expression of the person' (271). The significance of work for the person is that through work the human person develops their humanity and shares in the work of the Creator. In a real sense we 'image God' through participating creatively and responsibly in the ongoing task of creation (275). Indeed, through work we participate 'not only in the act of creation but also in that of redemption' (263).

The relationship between human work (labour) and capital has been the focus of debate and disagreement between competing world-views over the centuries. The Church's social doctrine has a very clear and consistent view of that relationship based on its understanding of the primacy of the person. Since the dignity and happiness of the human person is central to the vision of the Christian Gospel it must ultimately be the 'measuring stick' of capital and its uses. Consequently capital is subordinate to the human person and, indeed, must serve the human person-in-community. In the words of *Laborem exercens*, 'labour has a priority over capital' (277). Though both are needed, labour always has precedence since it is a human person who provides the labour.

The important question is whether capital and economic strategies serve the human person and contribute to the flourishing of the human family. In serving the human person the uses of capital must also respect and help realise the principle of the universal destination of the world's goods. This principle, which will be clarified in Part 3, boldly asserts that the world and its fruits were meant for all the human family.

According to Catholic social teaching, labour and capital are both needed in a relationship of complementarity. It is imperative therefore to construct economic systems where the opposition between capital and labour is overcome (277). They both serve the same goal of promoting the dignity of the person and the common good of society. It is equally true that both need to be critiqued by their response to that goal.

In the same encyclical Pope John Paul II argued strongly that we all share in 'two inheritances': firstly, the created world and its fruits, which have been given to all and are said to have 'a universal destination'; secondly, we have inherited the fruits of those generations that preceded us – their labour, insights and discoveries. These inheritances constitute the 'great workbench' on which humanity works. Today's workers through their effort and creativity contribute to this common workbench. Consequently the worker is 'fully entitled to consider him/herself a part-owner of the great workbench where s/he is working with everyone else' (281). It is only right and proper therefore that the participation of workers in management, ownership and profit be facilitated (281). This insight and demand of the Church's social doctrine has many creative possibilities. If acted upon it would give to workers a real sense of ownership of their work and remove some of the tension between workers and management.

Labour and private property

From the beginning of its social doctrine the Church has defended the right to private property as a natural right. In has vigorously defended this right against the claims of the communist system. However, it has never seen this right as an absolute right. Rather, the right to private property is subordinated to a more fundamental principle: the universal destination of goods. The world and its fruits were created for all of the human family. The use of private property must also facilitate the realisation of that principle. *Laborem exercens*, at paragraph 14, made this point with great clarity: 'The right to private property is subordinated to the right to common use, to the fact that goods are meant for everyone.'

Similarly the right to private property must be at the service of work since it is the fruit of work. This is especially true of the means of production and the goods proper to the world of finance, technology, knowledge and personnel. Public and private property must be 'orientated to an economy of service to humankind, so that they contribute to putting into effect the principle of the universal destination of the world's goods' (283). All property – including new technologies and knowledge – has a universal destination.

The creation of employment

Given the status of work – a fundamental right that gives expression to and enhances our dignity – full employment is a mandatory objective of every economic system orientated towards justice and the common good. Unemployment, on the other hand, must be seen as a 'real social disaster'. In combating unemployment a particular responsibility lies with the 'indirect employers', those who create and direct policies, at the local and international level, concerning labour and the economy (288). The State too has an important role in promoting the right to work by creating the conditions that ensure job opportunities (291). In a global economy it is imperative that the State works with other countries through agreements and cooperation to create the conditions that ensure the right to work.

Conditions of work

All those responsible for the creation of work – government, unions, business – must pay special heed to the rights of the family and the rights and dignity of women in the workforce. In particular there is a need to promote work policies that 'do not penalise but rather support the family nucleus' (294). Similarly the presence of women in the workplace must be both guaranteed and structured in a way that women 'do not have to pay for their advancement by abandoning what is specific to them' (294). The reality of many forms of discrimination against women in the workplace must be acknowledged and challenged, especially in the areas of pay, insurance and social security.

The reality of child labour (296) poses a significant moral problem for employers, states and consumers. There is clear evidence that some children still work in conditions of veritable slavery. Aid agencies and human rights organisations have done a great service to society by highlighting and combating this reality. This situation clearly infringes on the rights and dignity of children and compromises their blossoming. This point was clearly articulated by Pope Leo XIII as he confronted the horrors of the Industrial Revolution: 'For, just as very rough weather destroys the buds of spring, so does too early an experience of life's hard toil blight the young promise of a child's faculties ...' (296).

The problem of child labour is compounded by the fact that in some countries it makes an indispensable contribution to family income and the national economy. Individual states and international bodies, as well as non-governmental agencies, must strive to create the conditions that remove the need for child labour. Consumer groups can also play a vital role by demanding that the products they purchase are manufactured in conditions that are respectful of workers' rights and dignity. In this regard unjust trading relationships between the developed and developing world – that do not deliver just prices for raw material and labour – should be the focus of special attention.

Development agencies such as Trócaire have tried to overcome these obstacles to justice by promoting the Fair Trade movement as well as other initiatives. Fair Trade deals directly with small farmers and traders in the developing world and guarantees them a just price for their produce. Fair Trade produce, such as tea and coffee, is now available in many supermarkets and makes an important contribution to raising awareness about justice and solidarity. It also presents the consumer with a very practical way of promoting the rights and dignity of those living in great poverty.

Immigrants

In a global economy immigration is a reality in many countries. This reality should be seen as 'a resource for development rather than an obstacle to it'. It is incumbent on those who direct the economy to ensure that they do not exploit foreign labourers by denying them the same rights enjoyed by nationals. Rights, both in the area of employment and fundamental human rights, 'are to be guaranteed to all without discrimination' (298). The reality of immigration brings other challenges that demand a response from society. One such challenge is that of reuniting families separated by immigration. The Church's social doctrine argues that 'the right of reuniting families should be respected and promoted' (298). This demand flows naturally from the Church's understanding of the nature and rights of the family.

A right to strike?

The right to strike is unambiguously affirmed in Catholic social teaching since *Rerum Novarum* of Leo XIII. However, that right should only be exercised as a last resort when all other avenues have been exhausted and 'when it is necessary to obtain a proportionate benefit' (304). In the Church's social doctrine, unions are recognised as legitimate and necessary promoters of the struggle for social justice and defenders of 'the rights of workers in their particular professions' (306).

They contribute to the common good of society by encouraging and enabling a spirit of cooperation and justice in the workplace. In a changing world with increasing economic and financial globalisation, unions are challenged to show new forms of solidarity. This must involve offering protection not only to the traditional categories of workers but also to 'workers with non-standard or limited contracts, employees whose jobs are threatened by business mergers ... to immigrants, seasonal workers' (308).

Globalisation

Globalisation is seen as one of the 'new things' of the world of work (310–22) and brings with it both opportunities and challenges. The phenomenon of globalisation – where plants are located away from where strategies are decided and far from the markets where goods will be consumed – is driven by the extraordinary speed of communication today and the ease of movement of peoples and goods. In itself globalisation is neither good nor bad; it depends on how it is used. Like all realities in the economic and social sphere it must be evaluated in terms of its impact on the human person and the common good. From the perspective of the Church's social doctrine the great challenge is that the globalisation of the economy should lead to 'a globalisation of safeguards, minimum essential rights and equity' (310). Through the process of globalisation the rights and dignity of workers should be more universally recognised and protected. More specifically, the protections enjoyed by workers in most developed economies should be extended to all.

A new economy

Another of the 'new things' associated with today's global economy is the rapid move from an industrial-type economy to an economy essentially built on services and technological innovation. We have seen this phenomenon in Ireland and in other societies during the past decade of economic growth. In that time many new professions have enriched the world of work while some of the traditional professions and skills have all but disappeared (313). This change has often been accompanied by an era of transition from a culture of stable jobs to a 'universe of jobs where there is great variety, fluidity and a wealth of promises' (314). The notion of a permanent lifelong job is becoming obsolete in this era of transition and change.

These changes in the world of work bring with them many opportunities and challenges. Uncertainty and instability in the workplace can impact negatively on the person and family. However, decentralisation can lead to smaller companies being energised and can make the experience of work more 'human'. There is also the danger that in an economy of rapid change those working in the 'informal' and 'hidden' economies can be working in distressing conditions unworthy of their dignity as persons (316).

How do we evaluate these new realities in the world of work? The *Compendium* argues that 'the decisive factor and "referee" of this complex phase of change is once more the human person' (317). The subjective dimension of work must be recognised and protected worldwide. Work practices, old and new, must serve the integral development of the person and the common good of the whole human family.

Challenge: A new solidarity

The great challenge facing society in this era of change is the creation of a new solidarity that would include 'every region of the world including those less advantaged' (321). Such a response of solidarity would help create an authentically global development that would be inclusive and would help realise the principle that the earth and its riches were meant for all.

Pointers for further discussion

1 'The human person is the measure of the dignity of work: In fact there is no doubt that human work has an ethical value of its own, which clearly and directly remains linked to the fact that the one who carries it out is a person.' (271)

- What does it mean to you to say that 'the human person is the measure of the dignity of work'?

- The result of work is not just that the job gets done (ie. an objective good) but that through work a person expresses and develops themselves (ie. a subjective good). How can we promote this understanding of the subjective dimension of work in society?

- What are the particular challenges for society in integrating this vision into our work models and practices?

2 'The rights of workers, like all other rights, are based on the nature of the human person and on his/her transcendent dignity. The Church's social Magisterium has seen fit to list some of these rights ... the right to a just wage; the right to rest; the right to a working environment and to manufacturing processes which are not harmful to the workers' physical health or to their moral dignity; the right to assemble and form associations ...' (301)

- Why do you think these workers' rights were identified?

- Discuss how the workers' rights outlined here are respected in our society.

- Are there forces within society that seek to deny these rights? Why?

- Is the naming of workers' rights a valid concern for the Church? Who in the Church has the role of promoting such rights?

3 The 'historical forms in which human work is expressed change, but not its permanent requirements, which are summed up in the respect of the inalienable human rights of workers' (319).

- What are the particular challenges to workers and their rights posed by the present economic climate?

- Are there groups of workers who are particularly vulnerable in society today?

- How might we, as Christians, respond to their needs?

PART 3

The Basic Tools for a
Critical Evaluation of
the Social, Political and
Economic Spheres

Chapter Four

Catholic social teaching

Central principles

(Compendium Chapter 4)

As we have seen there is a vast and increasing volume of Catholic social teaching that addresses a wide range of issues – international debt, nuclear deterrence, international trade agreements, the ecological crisis – in the contemporary world. This teaching is generated by the universal and the local Church as it strives, in a systematic way, to apply the values of the Gospel to the social, economic and political realities of our day. Despite the volume and variety of Catholic social teaching and its dynamic nature it is possible to identify core principles that are universal and unchanging. These are the fundamental tools that enable the tradition to approach and critique the wide range of issues that have a bearing on the lives of individuals and communities. They also provide us with the tools to construct, in an imaginative and creative way, alternative strategies and priorities; alternatives that would impact more favourably on the rights of persons and communities.

1. THE UNIVERSAL DESTINATION OF THE WORLD'S GOODS (171–84)

A fundamental principle of the Christian world-view is that God created the world for everyone. All persons, created in the 'image of God', have been gifted with God's creation. The *Compendium* quotes *Gaudium et spes*:

God destined the earth and all it contains for all humankind and all peoples so that all created things would be shared fairly by all of humankind under the guidance of justice tempered by charity. (171)

Centesimus annus further affirmed and clarified this principle:

God gave the earth to the whole human race for the sustenance of all its members, without excluding or favouring anyone. This is the foundation of the universal destination of the earth's goods. (171)

Because the world was created for the benefit of all then each person has a *right* to use the goods of the earth. The scope of this right is determined by our needs. Each person 'must have access to the level of well-being necessary for his full development' (172). This insight provides a substantial principle with which to critique and evaluate developments in the areas of economics and politics. The right to use the earth's resources is a natural right, inscribed in human nature and not merely a positive right. It is intrinsic to the human person. It means that all other rights 'including property rights and the right of free trade must be subordinated to this norm [the universal destination of goods]; they must not hinder it, but must rather expedite its application' (172).

The principle of the universal destination of goods is an invitation to develop an economic vision inspired by moral values that does not 'lose sight of the origin or purpose of these goods, so as to bring about a world of fairness and solidarity' (174).

Private property

An important question to be raised at this stage is how the principle of the universal destination of the world's goods can be reconciled with the *right to private property*. This is an important question that the tradition has addressed and responded to over the centuries. The tradition holds that this right, though clearly affirmed as a natural right, is subordinate to the more fundamental right of all to share in the bounty of God's creation. It states that the Christian tradition has 'never recognised the right to private property as absolute and untouchable. On the contrary – the right to private property is subordinated to the right to common use, to the fact that goods are meant for everyone' (177). Indeed, the right to private property is not only subordinate to the more fundamental right but is at its service. Private property is in 'essence only an instrument for respecting the principle of the universal destination of goods; in the final analysis, therefore, it is not an end but a means' (177).

The Church's social doctrine has always emphasised the social function of private property. Individual persons should not use their resources 'without considering the effects that this use will have, rather they must act in a way that benefits not only themselves and their family but also the common good' (178). The right to private property, as a lesser right, can be limited if it does not facilitate the recognition and concrete expression of the more fundamental principle. This point was clearly made in paragraph 25 of the encyclical *Populorum progressio* where it argued that if landed estates impede the general prosperity of a nation the 'common good sometimes demands their expropriation'. The encyclical accepted that this could be the case if the lands were unused, poorly used or detrimental to the interests of the country.

In the present historical period the principle of the universal destination of the goods of the earth must be extended to include the 'new goods' which are the result of knowledge, technology and know-how. This is critically important because increasingly 'the wealth of the industrial nations is based much more on this kind of ownership than on natural resources' (179). Technology and expertise is the new raw material that generates wealth and development. These goods too are part of a shared human inheritance and should be made available to all peoples.

Preferential option for the poor

The principle of the universal destination of goods has immediate and obvious implications for how we engage with the poor and marginalised. In the Church's eyes it demands a particular stance, what it calls a 'preferential option for the poor'. Those whose 'living conditions interfere with their proper growth should be the focus of particular concern' (182). This stance should impact decisively on the Church's priorities, strategies and values. Concern for the poor and disadvantaged is a central demand of the Gospel and must be a priority for all Christians.

Mt 25:40

I tell you solemnly, in so far as you did this to one of the least of these brothers and sisters of mine, you did it to me.

This vision has inspired Christian individuals and groups throughout the centuries who have responded with energy and generosity. Groups such as the St Vincent de Paul Society and Trócaire are just two examples of Gospel-inspired organisations that have made the plight of the disadvantaged their special concern. This 'preferential option for the poor' must, however, be a challenge for and characteristic of the whole Church and should be reflected in pastoral priorities as well as in lifestyles. The challenge to 'live simply so that others may simply live' is a concrete expression of this 'preferential option for the poor'.

II. THE COMMON GOOD OF SOCIETY AND HUMANITY (164–70)

The common good is understood in the Church's social doctrine to be: 'the sum total of social conditions which allow people, either as groups or as individuals, to reach their fulfilment more fully and more easily' (164). The common good of society could be described as the ethos or fabric of society. It provides the context or environment that enables people to blossom and achieve their potential. It is rooted in the dignity, unity and equality of all people. Societies that wish to serve the human person see the common good as their primary goal. This principle provides a robust critique of rugged individualism. It understands the human person as a person-in-community and moderates the exercise of individual freedom by appealing to the well-being of others and of the community.

Everyone in society has a responsibility towards the common good but the political community has a unique and indispensable role. This was clearly highlighted in pastoral letters by the English and Welsh Catholic Bishops in which they identified the common good as the key issue to be addressed at election time.[1] Citizens have a responsibility to determine how the economic and social policies of a political party or individual impact on the common good of society. After conscientious consideration they should vote for the politicians or policies which they judge best promote the common good.

---

1   Catholic Bishops' Conference of England & Wales, *The Common Good and the Church's Social Teaching*, 1996 and *Vote for the Common Good*, 2001. Both are available at www.catholic-ew.org.uk/ie

It is important that the content of the common good be understood in a wholesome way that includes its transcendent dimension (170). Christian anthropology understands the human person as more than one-dimensional. God is our origin and destiny and a relationship with God is an essential requirement of the human person. To reduce the common good to socio-economic well-being only would not contribute to or enable human flourishing. The human drive to seek religious truth and to live by that truth must be included in any adequate understanding of the common good.

Finally, the common good must be understood in its global dimensions. Individual nations and communities must pursue the common good of the whole human family and not just that of a particular society or people. Nations must question how the policies and strategies they pursue impact on the global family. Do they enable the flourishing of the many or the few? This perspective – the global common good – provides the ultimate critique of economic and social policies pursued by national and international bodies.

III. THE PRINCIPLE OF SUBSIDIARITY (185-8)

This principle states that the State should not take to itself functions and roles that the individual person and organisations can do for themselves. It recognises that families, groups and associations – sports, cultural, political, social – make a necessary and invaluable contribution to the life of society. In this they should be encouraged and supported.

The role of the State should be to help (*subsidium*) rather than replace or control these groups and organisations as they contribute to the richness and vibrancy of life in society.

The principle of subsidiarity was identified in *Quadragesimo Anno* in 1931 as a most 'important principle of social philosophy' (186). Pope Pius XI was alert to the danger of the individual person and social groups being absorbed by the all-powerful state. This was a real possibility in the historical context out of which the encyclical emerged. Pope Pius had witnessed the emergence of totalitarian regimes that paid scant attention to the rights of the individual and family. Freedom, personal initiative and responsibility were compromised by state intervention and control.

The content of the principle is that the initiative, freedom and responsibility of the individual and the smaller essential cells in society must not be supplanted. In a positive sense the principle highlights the duty of the State to help individuals and social groups to fulfil their duties. Underlying the principle is a recognition that 'every person, family and intermediate group has something original to offer to the community' (187).

The denial of subsidiarity limits and even destroys the spirit of freedom and initiative. The *Compendium* identifies the following realities where the principle is denied: 'certain forms of centralisation, bureaucratisation and welfare assistance and the unjustified and excessive presence of the State in public mechanisms' (187). The human person and society are ultimately diminished if the zone of personal responsibility, freedom and initiative is unduly restricted.

However, the flourishing of the individual and of society is facilitated when there is respect for the person, an appreciation of associations, the encouragement of private initiative, bureaucratic and administrative decentralisation, a balance struck between public and private spheres, and when citizens are encouraged in actively 'being a part' of the political and social reality of their country (187).

The principle of subsidiarity does not of course exclude the intervention of the State in the life of society. It does rather provide a principle of balance that ensures that the person and groups in society are not denied their rightful freedom, initiative and responsibility. The State must at times take a more proactive and central role in the life of society by, for example, stimulating the economy or creating equality when these projects are unable to be realised by individuals and civil society on their own.

The principle of subsidiarity got an airing in Ireland during the infamous Mother and Child controversy in the early 1950s.[2] The Catholic Bishops argued that the health scheme proposed by Dr Noel Browne was contrary to this principle of Catholic teaching by giving to the State a role and function that the individual and family could provide for themselves. Such a scheme by providing State health care for all mothers would, it was claimed, damage personal initiative and responsibility. From the perspective of today the application of the principle to this case seems at least strained if not entirely misplaced.

IV. THE IMPORTANCE OF PARTICIPATION (189–91)

Participation in society is seen as a basic right and a duty of all towards the common good of society. It is closely linked to the principle of subsidiarity and could be seen as an inevitable consequence of that principle.

---

2   See J.H. Whyte, *Church and State in Modern Ireland 1923–1979,* 2nd edn, Gill and Macmillan, 1980, Chapters 7, 8 and Appendix B.

Participation is understood as a 'series of activities by means of which the citizen contributes to the cultural, economic, political and social life of the civil community to which he belongs' (189). Participation is one of the pillars of 'all democratic orders and one of the major guarantees of the permanence of the democratic system' (190). The Church's social doctrine is critical of totalitarian or dictatorial regimes because 'the fundamental right to participate in public life is denied at its origin, since it is considered a threat to the State itself' (191).

Because participation is a basic right that contributes to the common good of society there is a duty on all to challenge attitudes and structures that work against participation. Voting is an obvious and essential way for the citizen to participate in the life of society. Through voting in a conscientious way the citizen assumes moral responsibility for the common good of society. In this regard abstaining from voting must be seen as the dereliction of duty.

V. THE PRINCIPLE AND VIRTUE OF SOLIDARITY (192–196)

The principle of solidarity 'highlights in a particular way the intrinsic social nature of the human person, the equality of all in dignity and rights and the common path of individuals and people towards an ever more committed unity' (192). It strives to make the oneness of our humanity the foundation for shared action for the betterment of all peoples.

This generation lives in a time that has made us increasingly aware of the bond of interdependence between individuals and peoples. Modern communications, and especially the use of computers and the internet, have made the global village a reality in our everyday experiences. We can easily be

Mk 10:43-45

This is not to happen among you. No; anyone who wants to become great among you must be your servant, and anyone who wants to be first among you must be slave to all. For the Son of Man himself did not come to be served but to serve, and give his life as a ransom for many.

Catholic social teaching

immersed in the joys and tragedies of others even when they live on the other side of the globe. It could be argued that the reality of our shared humanity is confirmed, or at least made more difficult to deny, through these modern means of communication.

Unfortunately the power of instant worldwide communication has also highlighted stark inequalities between peoples. The gap in living standards between and within the developed and developing world is readily seen on our TV screens. So too is the reality of unjust trading contracts between nations. The challenge, therefore, is to move the reality of our shared humanity and interdependence into the ethical and social plane.

In the Church's social doctrine solidarity is understood both as a 'social principle and a moral virtue' (193). It challenges us to engage the structures of sin that perpetuate injustice. These must be transformed into structures of solidarity that facilitate the development of all of humanity. This transformation can be achieved by the modification of laws, market regulations and juridical systems so that they enable justice, inclusion and integral human development to be a reality for all. Solidarity is an authentic moral virtue and not just a 'feeling of vague compassion or shallow distress at the misfortunes of so many people' (193). It involves a firm determination to commit oneself to 'the good of all and of each individual, because we are all really responsible for all' (193).

Christians in embracing the virtue of solidarity, as a response to our shared humanity, are further inspired by the example of Christ, who calls us to serve our neighbour. The Christian vision furthermore calls and challenges us to see the 'neighbour', wherever they may be, as a 'living image of God' and as Christ in our midst.

VI. THE FUNDAMENTAL VALUES OF SOCIAL LIFE (197–208)

The Church, as a living and dynamic community of people striving to live the Gospel in changing times, has identified values that are essential for building and maintaining a humane society. These are the essential core values that should inspire individuals and the civil authorities in their service of society and the common good. They are truth, freedom, justice and love.

Truth

It is part of the human condition to seek the truth about the reality we call life. What is the truth of the human person? What is the meaning of the world we live in? What is the truth about morality? These are fundamental questions that engage people from an early age. This searching and questioning is an essential dimension of being human. Consequently, all persons have the right and duty to search for and live by the truth, and this right must be recognised and facilitated by the State in its service of the human person (198).

Today, unfortunately, many have become sceptical about the possibility of knowing the truth and have abandoned the search. Others have adopted a relativism that denies the reality of 'objective truth' and encourages all to have their own version of the truth. For the Christian these stances are false and consequently inadequate as foundations for individual or societal life. There are 'objective' truths about human nature and morality that can be known and which provide the foundations for a wholesome society. Therefore, society should encourage the search for and discussion about these truths.

Freedom

A cursory glance through the history of the Church clearly indicates that the value of human freedom was not always fully appreciated. The Inquisition, the Syllabus of Errors and the denial of religious freedom come readily to mind as examples of the Church's strained relationship with human freedom.

Today the Church is a firm advocate of human freedom as the highest sign of our creation 'in the divine image and, consequently, is a sign of the sublime dignity of every human person' (199). Freedom is an essential part of the human condition and we all have a natural right to have that freedom recognised. Furthermore, the exercise of freedom, 'especially in moral and religious matters, is an inalienable requirement of the dignity of the human person' (199). Through the exercise of freedom we constitute ourselves as persons; we give a shape and direction to our lives.

The *Compendium* contains a list of freedoms (200) that flow naturally from our nature as human persons. These include the right to seek the truth and to express our religious, cultural and political ideas, the right to express one's opinions and to choose one's state of life.

Freedom, like all rights exercised in society, is not an absolute right and therefore can be restricted. In the first instance we are called to be responsible moral agents and to exercise our freedom with due regard to the rights of others and the moral law. The responsible use of freedom then challenges each individual in their exercise of freedom. The State, in its service of the community, also has a legitimate role in placing limits on the exercise of freedom. It must limit freedom, even religious freedom, if it is damaging of the 'common good and public order' of society (200).

Justice

According to an ancient and hallowed formulation, justice 'consists in the constant and firm will to give their due to God and neighbour' (201). It is translated into behaviour 'that is based on the will to recognise the other as a person' (201) with rights and entitlements. It constitutes the decisive criterion of morality in the inter-subjective and social sphere. The Church has traditionally distinguished between commutative, distributive and legal justice. Today a great importance is given to social justice which 'concerns the social, political and economic aspects and, above all, the structural dimension of problems and their respective solutions' (201).

In the Christian tradition justice is rooted in a respect for the nature and dignity of the human person. As such it cannot be reduced to conformity to a law or contract but must open itself to solidarity and love.

Love

In the Christian vision love presupposes and transcends justice (206). Human relations cannot be governed solely by the measure of justice. Justice must, so to speak, be 'corrected' to a considerable extent by that love which, as St Paul proclaims, 'is patient and kind'. It must also possess the characteristics of that merciful love that is at the heart of the Gospel.

1 Cor 13:13

In short there are three things that last: faith, hope and love; and the greatest of these is love.

The history of humanity clearly indicates that no legislation, system of rules or negotiation is ever adequate to persuade individuals and nations to live in 'unity, brotherhood and peace' (207). Only love can ultimately transform persons, change attitudes and renew societies. Laws and regulations make an invaluable contribution but it is our attitude, how we see and respond to 'the other', that will ultimately transform society.

Pointers for further discussion

1 'A society that wishes and intends to remain at the service of the human being at every level is a society that has the common good – the good of all people and of the whole person – as its primary goal.' (165)

- Discuss the term 'the common good'. What does it mean? Is it more than socio-economic well-being?

- Who has responsibility for promoting the common good?

- What is the particular contribution that the Church can make, in your parish or globally, to the promotion of the common good?

2 'God gave the earth to the whole human race for the sustenance of all its members, without excluding or favouring anyone. This is the foundation of the universal destination of the earth's goods.' (171)

- In a very divided world what can you do to ensure that the whole human race enjoys the fruits of the earth?

- Do we in the developed world need to change our lifestyles and consumer choices in order that others may live?

- Is it overly optimistic to believe that the earth can and should provide for everyone? What needs to change in society for this to become feasible?

3 'It is therefore clearly evident that every democracy must be participative. This means that the different subjects of civil community at every level must be informed, listened to and involved in the exercise of the carried-out functions.' (190)

- Can you identify the ways in which society today ensures that people at 'every level' of our civil community are informed, listened to and involved?

- The Church affirms participation in society as a central demand of the Church's social doctrine. Why do you think the Church values participation so highly?

- How can Christian citizens live out their duty to participate in the cultural and social life of the community to which they belong?

- Can you imagine and describe a society where everyone participates fully? What do you learn about today's society when you do this imagining?

4 'The message of the Church's social doctrine regarding solidarity clearly shows that there exists an intimate bond between solidarity and the common good, between solidarity and the universal destination of goods, between solidarity and equality among men/women and peoples, between solidarity and peace in the world.' (194)

- Discuss the word 'solidarity'. What does it mean in concrete terms? What expressions of solidarity do you see in your local community?

- Find ways to describe in your own words what it means to say that 'solidarity is a principle and a virtue'. What is the central value that is at the foundation of such solidarity?

- How can we build the principle and virtue of solidarity into our everyday decisions and actions, both at home and in the community/parish?

5 'All social values are inherent in the dignity of the human person, whose authentic development they foster. Essentially, these values are: truth, freedom, justice, love. Putting them into practice is the sure and necessary way of obtaining personal perfection and a more human social existence.' (197)

- Where do you notice the values of truth, freedom, justice and love being lived out in society today?

- Can you see and share with others how you live them out in your own life?

- Who is responsible for the implementation of these values in the Church and in society?

- The Church is called to proclaim and live out these values. How do you see this being done at an international, national and local level?

PART 4

The Application of the Principles of Catholic Social Doctrine to the Economic, Political and Social Spheres

Chapter Five

Economic life

(*Compendium* Chapter 7)

The economy and economic systems play a very important role in our individual lives and in the life of society. They have an impact on the present and they help shape the future. The Christian community in its service of the person-in-community asks some important questions about the economy. What criteria should we use to evaluate economic systems and theories? Is there one particular economic system that is more in harmony with the Christian vision?

The Christian narrative does not explicitly deal with economics and so does not provide us with explicit and unambiguous answers to some of these questions. It does, however, provide us with a vision that gives us fundamental principles and values that can guide our activity in the sphere of economics as it does in all other areas of life. The scriptures highlight the importance of honesty, justice and care for others. These are important values that enable us to critique economic systems and programmes. Today, Christian discipleship involves continuing the work of Jesus by conforming our actions, both individual and societal, and structures to those of the Gospel. In the Gospel vision, wealth exists to be shared (328) and economic activity is directed to serve the good of persons.

Mt 6:24

No one can be the slave of two masters: he will either hate the first and love the second, or treat the first with respect and the second with scorn. You cannot be the slave both of God and of money.

Morality and the economy

Economics, like all human activities, must be exercised within parameters set by the moral law. Though an independent discipline with its own history, foundational principles and expertise, it can never be understood to be independent of morality. The Church's social doctrine argues that the human person 'is the source, the centre and the purpose of all economic and social life' (331). The need for economic activity to be limited by the demands of morality was very clearly articulated by Pope John Paul II, in the encyclical *Centesimus annus*, when he reflected on the historic events of 1989 that resulted in the collapse of communism. An obvious question in many minds was whether capitalism would now be promoted, by the Pope, as 'the way'. The response of Pope John Paul II to this question is critical and nuanced:

If by 'capitalism' is meant an economic system which recognises the fundamental and positive role of business, the market, private property and the resulting responsibility for the means of production, as well as free human creativity in the economic sector, then the answer is certainly in the affirmative … But, if by 'capitalism' is meant a system in which freedom in the economic sector is not circumscribed within a strong juridical framework which places it at the service of human freedom in its totality, and which sees it as a particular aspect of that freedom, the core of which is ethical and religious, then the reply is certainly negative. (335)

Here, Pope John Paul II emphatically rejects 'rigid' capitalism that only recognises the dynamics and limits of market forces. He accepts a model of capitalism that is limited and regulated by the demands of the human person and the common good of the human family. Specifically capitalism must be at the service of the demands of human dignity and the principle of the universal destination of the world's goods.

Economic activity must, therefore, be directed towards 'human development in solidarity'. It must also concern itself with identifying and tackling 'structures of sin' which generate and perpetuate poverty, underdevelopment and degradation. From the perspective of the Christian vision these structures enshrine attitudes and goals that are sinful or disordered. It is important to recognise that these 'sinful structures' – laws, economic policies, trade agreements – are not beyond human control but are rather constructed and maintained by human persons. They are the result of human choices that reflect concrete acts of human selfishness, greed or, indeed, indifference to the plight of others. The 'good news' is that these same structures can be transformed through human activity to reflect more perfectly Gospel values and so contribute to human flourishing.

Private initiative and business initiative

The freedom of the person in economic matters is a fundamental value and an inalienable right to be promoted and defended (336). Business serves the common good of society through the production of useful goods and services. The Church's social doctrine insists that business is not just a 'society of capital goods' but a 'society of persons' and that the care and well-being of the person must be central to the ethos of business. In this regard, though profit is the first indicator that business is functioning well, it is not, on its own, an adequate criterion. Profit can often be generated at the expense of the dignity of the workers and the common good of society. Usury is cited as one such example that results in great human misery (341). The legitimate pursuit of profit should, rather, be carried out in a manner that is in harmony with the dignity of the person.

Role of the State

The free market has historically shown itself to be the best in honouring the demands of human initiative and sustained economic growth. However, there is also a vital role for the State in the domain of economics. The intervention of the State, in its service of the common good, should be governed by the principles of Solidarity and Subsidiarity (351). Both principles are needed for an intervention that is wholesome. Solidarity on its own can lead to a welfare state that ultimately diminishes personal initiative and responsibility. Subsidiarity on its own can generate a 'self-centred localism' that loses sight of the common good. The State in its service of the common good provides the environment – stability, a juridical framework, laws, stable currency – which enables business to thrive.

Globalisation

Globalisation, as one of the 'new things' in the economic sector, has the potential to produce benefits for the whole human family. We have already seen the challenges and opportunities it brings to the world of work. Similar challenges and opportunities exist in the area of the economy. There is plenty of evidence available today that globalisation is contributing to 'increasing inequalities' between and within nations. The challenge is to ensure a globalisation in 'solidarity, a globalisation without marginalisation' (363). The fact that access to new technologies is uneven contributes to these increasing inequalities.

In many instances the economic gap is often accompanied by a gap in human rights promotion and protection. In advanced societies 'new rights' are being promoted while, at the same time, more fundamental rights – the right to food and drinkable water, to housing and security, to self-determination – are ignored in less prosperous nations (365). This reality indicates that the process of globalisation must be monitored and directed so that it contributes to solidarity and inclusion rather than exclusion. It must also be directed so that it avoids the temptation of becoming 'a new version of colonialism'. In this regard respect for the diversity of cultures, including religious beliefs, is essential (366).

The phenomenon of globalisation can also limit the effectiveness of nation states in directing their national economic systems. The reality is that many nation states are smaller and less powerful than the giant multi-national companies. This has the potential to do great damage to the global common good. Consequently, there is a vital role for the international community and agencies to 'exercise a strong guiding role' that directs economic activity towards the 'goal of attaining the common good of the whole human family' (371). Those involved in international economic activity are challenged, particularly, to recognise the interdependence of peoples, the need to develop solidarity and to move beyond an individualistic culture.

Finally, in the Christian vision of life economic activity cannot be made into an absolute. It is just one dimension of life. Though it contributes to the development of society it does not ensure the integral development of the person and community. Such development can only be assured when the needs of the whole person – including the spiritual – are attended to. The Christian vision of the human person – Christian anthropology – further implies that the material and instinctive dimensions of the person are at the service of the interior and spiritual ones (376).

Lk 12:21

So it is when a man stores up treasure for himself in place of making himself rich in the sight of God.

Pointers for further discussion

1 'The moral dimension of the economy shows that economic efficiency and the promotion of human development in solidarity are not two separate or alternative aims but one indivisible goal.' (332)

- Discuss how 'economic efficiency' and 'the promotion of human development in solidarity' can be 'one indivisible goal'.

- If the economy has a moral dimension who can best offer a critique of the economy and economic policies? And how?

- Can you highlight ways in which the goal of 'human development in solidarity' is promoted in today's economy?

2 'Business owners and management must not limit themselves to taking into account only the economic objectives of the company ... It is also their precise duty to respect concretely the human dignity of those who work within the company. These workers constitute "the firm's most valuable asset" and the decisive factor of production.' (344)

- In your workplace are you the 'most valuable asset'?

- Do you see others in this way?

- In what ways can businesses and organisations ensure the promotion of human dignity in the way they do their business?

- What are the threats to this vision of the workplace in a highly competitive economy?

3 'Globalisation gives rise to new hopes while at the same time it poses troubling questions. Globalisation is able to produce potentially beneficial effects for the whole of humanity.' (362)

- Globalisation is a very familiar word today. Discuss what you understand by the term.

- What are the challenges and opportunities that accompany the increasing globalisation of the economy?

- What are the local actions that can positively contribute to economic globalisation?

Chapter Six
Political life

It is immediately obvious that the Christian scriptures have little explicit reference to the world of politics or to political theories. Revelation does, however, provide us with principles and values that we can apply to the contemporary world of politics. The foundational insight it gives us is that of Christian anthropology; how we understand and value the human person.

Purpose and limits of the political community

From the perspective of the Christian tradition, the human person is the foundation and purpose of political life (384). The political community exists to achieve the full growth of each member of society and to serve the common good (384). It does this primarily by promoting and defending fundamental and inalienable human rights (388) and by creating an environment where people can exercise their rights and fulfil their duties.

Political authority (393–405) must be guided by the moral law and must respect, recognise and promote essential human and moral values. Though we can legitimately speak of the 'autonomy' of the political order this cannot mean freedom from the demands of objective morality. The consent of the people in a democracy, therefore, is not sufficient to make actions 'good' or 'just'. The moral status of actions or policies is determined with reference to objective morality and, in particular, the demands of human dignity and the common good.

With regard to civil laws or precepts that contravene the moral law the conscientious rights of citizens must be recognised. The right to conscientious objection is a basic human right that the civil law is obliged to protect. Those who have 'recourse to conscientious objection must be protected not only from legal penalties but also from any negative effects on the legal, disciplinary, financial and professional plane' (399).

Death penalty

In its service of the common good the lawful authorities must protect society from those who engage in criminal activity. It 'must exercise the right and duty to inflict punishment according to the seriousness of the crimes committed' (402). At all times the dignity of prisoners must be respected. Trials should be conducted swiftly, fairly and transparently. The demands of human dignity exclude acts of torture (404) or other deprivations while prisoners are in custody.

In recent decades there has been a growing opposition to the death penalty in the Christian community and beyond. This change in attitude is seen clearly in the content of Catholic teaching. The encyclical *Evangelium vitae* argues that the death penalty should only be used if it is absolutely necessary to safeguard the common good of society and the rights of individuals. Given the legal and penal systems in existence in most countries it emphasises that such occasions are 'very rare, if not practically non-existent'. The use of 'bloodless means' is more in conformity with the dignity of the human person and contributes to a more consistent ethic of life. The lives of all – the virtuous and the sinful – are sacred and worthy of our protection. This growing opposition to the death penalty is seen as a sign of hope (405) of an increase in respect for the dignity of every human person.

The democratic system

The question is often asked whether democracy is the political system most in harmony with the insights and values of the Gospel. The encyclical *Centesimus annus* contains an explicit and articulate judgement with regard to democracy that is quoted in the *Compendium*.

The Church values the democratic system inasmuch as it ensures the participation of citizens in making political choices, guarantees to the governed the possibility both of electing and holding accountable those who govern them, and of replacing them through peaceful means when appropriate. (406)

Authentic democracy is rooted in the dignity of every human person, respect for human rights and commitment to the common good. Though the Church speaks highly of democracy and its positive contribution to the well-being of individuals and societies it is also conscious of some of the dangers implicit in the democratic system.

One such danger is that of ethical relativism, which denies the existence of objective morality. Indeed, some claim that 'agnosticism and sceptical relativism are the philosophy and the basic attitude which correspond to democratic forms of political life' (407). The Church's social doctrine rejects both ethical relativism and its identification with the essence of democracy. It stresses that morality is both objective and knowable through reason and that democratic institutions are obliged to conform to its demands.

Furthermore, the Church's social doctrine contends that the 'moral' status of democracy is not automatic. Democracy is not 'good' or 'bad' in the abstract. Rather it 'depends on the morality of the ends which it pursues and of the means which it employs' (407).

Since the political community finds its purpose in the human person it is also at the service of civil society (417–20). It should encourage and facilitate the role of volunteer organisations and cooperative endeavours in society. In this way it contributes to the common good of society. In this engagement with society the State should respect the principle of subsidiarity (419) by encouraging and enabling the participation of citizens rather than replacing it.

The political community, in its commitment to the human person, has a special role to play in promoting and defending the right to religious freedom in society. The recognition of this right as a fundamental human right has been part of Catholic moral and social teaching since Vatican II. The right to religious freedom is rooted in the nature of the human person and the nature of the quest for religious truth. The truth cannot be imposed on anyone 'except by virtue of its own truth' (421). This right must be recognised as a fundamental civil right and its exercise must be facilitated by the State. The exercise of religious freedom in society – like most rights – is not of course an absolute right; its exercise can be limited by the civil authorities by appeal to the rights of others, the demands of justice and the common good.

The Catholic Church and the political community

What kind of relationship can there be between the Church and the political community? The shape of any such relationship will, in the first place, have to respect the nature and purpose of both. They are mutually independent and self-governing and pursue different ends. Their relationship should be marked by mutual respect and cooperation. Since both serve the human person and community they can work together on a great variety of projects and policies. Their autonomy therefore does not entail 'a separation that excludes cooperation' (425).

The political community must give the Church space to carry out her mission of proclaiming the Gospel. The Church on her part must 'respect the legitimate autonomy of the democratic order' (424). However, the Church always retains the right, in its service of the human person, to question the religious and moral content of political programmes. In this it is only being true to its own self-understanding as the promoter of Gospel values in the world.

Pointers for further discussion

1   'Authority must recognise, respect and promote essential human and moral values. These are innate and "flow from the very truth of the human being and express and safeguard the dignity of the person; values which no individual, no majority and no State can ever create, modify or destroy".' (397)

- Do you agree with this statement? Why? Why not?

- Can you identify any experiences in human history when such 'human and moral values' were not recognised by a majority or a State? Can you see this happening in the world today?

- What is the foundation on which political life is built?

- Does this foundation place limits on the scope and freedom of political authority?

2 'Citizens are not obliged in conscience to follow the prescriptions of civil authorities if their precepts are contrary to the demands of the moral order, to the fundamental rights of persons or to the teachings of the Gospel.' (399)

- Consider and discuss examples where it might be right for a citizen to refuse 'to follow the prescriptions of civil authority'.
- What is the basis of this stance of the Church on the rights of conscience?
- Does this infringe on the 'autonomy' of the State?
- How do you see the Church and the State managing the relationship between freedom of conscience and legitimate civil authority in society today?

3 'An authentic democracy is not merely the result of a formal observation of a set of rules but is the fruit of a convinced acceptance of the values that inspire democratic procedures: the dignity of every human person, the respect of human rights, commitment to the common good as the purpose and guiding criterion for political life.' (407)

- Do we have an 'authentic democracy' in our country today?
- Is this vision of the roots and goals of democracy at work in our society?
- What are the responsibilities of citizens in general and of Christians specifically in an 'authentic democracy'?

- Is there some practical action that your group or parish could take to help build up our democracy?

Chapter Seven

The reality of global conflict and the challenge of peace

(Compendium Chapter 11)

In the Christian vision the promotion of peace flows readily from our self-understanding as a community centred on the person of Christ. Peace is central to the ethos and spirit of the Gospel narrative and the promotion of peace is understood as a duty that makes a demand on everyone. It must be seen as a positive reality, not just the absence of war or the maintenance of power between enemies. Peace is ultimately founded on a 'correct understanding of the human person and requires the establishment of an order based on justice and charity' (494).

Lk 10:5

Whatever house you go into, let your first words be, 'Peace to this house'.

In a broken and sinful world peace is threatened in many different ways. A lack of respect for human dignity often triggers conflict and hostility. The defence and promotion of human rights is therefore essential if we want to ensure peace. Likewise, since structural injustice and poverty are at the root of many conflicts, there is an obligation to promote justice and development worldwide (498).

In the Christian family there has always been two traditions with regard to the morality of war. The older tradition – Christian pacifism – held that fidelity to the Gospels and the person of Christ excluded any recourse to war and killing. The later and dominant tradition – the 'just war' tradition – argued that in a sinful and imperfect world recourse to war could be justified in certain circumstances. That tradition laid down strict guidelines that governed entry into war and conduct in war. The adequacy and relevance of the 'just war' tradition in an era of weapons of mass destruction is questioned by many today.

The Church in its pronouncements, especially in recent decades, has emphasised the contradiction between war and the Gospel ethos. From the perspective of the Gospel violence is never a proper response. It is always 'a lie, for it goes against the truth of our faith, the truth of our humanity. Violence destroys what it claims to defend: the dignity, the life, the freedom of human beings' (496). Pope John Paul II boldly proclaimed that war 'is always a defeat for humanity' (497). Consequently there is an urgent need for Christians and people of goodwill to seek alternatives to war as a solution to international conflict.

Though the Church's tradition views war as a defeat for humanity it acknowledges that each nation has the right and duty to defend itself against an unjust aggressor. This has been a consistent part of the 'just war' tradition. The *Compendium* quotes the Catechism of the Catholic Church when outlining the conditions that would justify a nation defending itself against an aggressor.

These conditions are:

the damage inflicted by the aggressor on the nation or community of nations must be lasting, grave and certain; all other means of putting an end to it must have been shown to be impractical or ineffective; there must be serious prospects of success; the use of arms must not produce evils and disorders graver than the evil to be eliminated. (500)

The application of these conditions to a concrete situation 'belongs to the prudential judgement of those who have responsibility for the common good' (500). In the international debate over the morality of the Iraq war there was debate among Catholic bishops, theologians and others as to whether these criteria were satisfied. In this regard the Catholic moral tradition accepts that people may disagree on the application of 'just war' criteria to concrete and complex situations. Though there is certainty and clarity about the fundamental principles (for example, non-combatant immunity) and values (respect for human life), there may be disagreement as to how these are honoured in a particular context.

The question of the morality of a pre-emptive strike featured prominently in the debate on the morality of the war in Iraq. On that issue the *Compendium* concludes that 'engaging in a preventive war without clear proof that an attack is imminent cannot fail to raise serious moral and juridical questions' (501).

In defending peace the armed forces of a country serve the cause of peace and the well-being of society (502). Within the defence forces it is imperative that individual members take responsibility for their actions. They cannot abandon personal responsibility 'by claiming obedience to the orders of superiors' (503). Given the contribution the defence forces make to the common good of society, by serving the cause of peace and justice, should there be an obligation on all citizens to join the armed forces in time of crisis? How should those who have conscientious objections be treated?

In modern times the Church's teaching has recognised the rights of conscientious objectors to war in general or to a particular war. These rights should be respected by the State 'provided they accept some other form of community service' (503). Citizens should be allowed to fulfil their responsibility to society in a manner that is in harmony with their religious and moral convictions. The Church's defence of the rights of conscientious objectors flows primarily from its understanding of the dignity of conscience. Everyone has the right and duty to seek moral and religious truth and to live by that truth. No one should be coerced into acting in a way that contradicts their conscientious insights. The acceptance of Christian pacifism as a legitimate moral stance also contributes to the Church's defence of conscientious objectors.

The duty to protect the innocent

A nation's right to legitimate defence is linked to its duty to protect those who cannot defend themselves (504). This duty must not be understood narrowly but must extend to refugees and ethnic groups who are under threat. Though the international community has a special role and duty in this area, individual states cannot remain indifferent to the plight of the innocent outside their borders. The principle of national sovereignty cannot be claimed as a 'motive for preventing an intervention in defence of innocent victims' (506). Individual states must accept their responsibilities for the protection of the innocent.

The role of sanctions?

Sanctions can be used by the international community against those who threaten peace but must be evaluated on an ongoing basis in terms of their impact on the civilian population. In particular, sanctions cannot be used in an indiscriminate way or as direct punishment of an entire population. It is 'not licit that entire populations, and above all their most vulnerable members, be made to suffer because of such sanctions' (507). Economic sanctions must be used with great discernment and must be subject to strict legal and ethical criteria.

Stockpiling of arms

The Church's social doctrine recognises that the stockpiling of arms poses a real threat to peace and to the promotion of justice. It also constitutes a destructive use of both the earth's resources and human creativity and genius. The use of vast resources to stockpile arms, given the reality of global poverty and deprivation, also has implications at the level of justice and human solidarity. Therefore, nations when exercising the right and duty of self-defence should depend on the 'principle of sufficiency' (508). On the question of disarmament, the Church's social doctrine 'proposes the goal of general, balanced and controlled disarmament' (508) rather than a policy of unilateral disarmament.

Nuclear deterrence and use

The question of the morality of nuclear deterrence was the subject of much discussion in the 1980s. At that time Pope John Paul II gave a 'conditional acceptance' to such deterrence once it was used as a means to securing peace and achieving disarmament. He rejected nuclear deterrence when pursued as an end it itself. The *Compendium* states that 'policies of nuclear deterrence ... must be replaced with concrete measures of disarmament based on dialogue and multilateral negotiations' (508). In recent months the Bishops of Scotland have contributed energetically to this debate on the morality of nuclear deterrence. They were responding to the decision by the British government to update its nuclear fleet.

The use of nuclear weapons is judged by most to fail the 'just war' criteria of 'non-combatant immunity' and 'proportionality'. In a memorable text Vatican II explicitly stated that the use of weapons that were 'aimed indiscriminately at the destruction of entire cities or extensive areas along with their population is a crime against God and man himself. It merits unequivocal and unhesitating condemnation' (509). Given the destructive and indiscriminate nature of nuclear weaponry this condemnation would seem to preclude any and every use of nuclear weapons.

Terrorism

The *Compendium* is unequivocal in its condemnation of terrorism and views it as 'one of the most brutal forms of violence traumatising the international community' (513). Such acts not only result in the loss of innocent lives but also sow seeds of hatred and a desire for revenge. In this way they inflict deep wounds on the common good of humanity.

The Christian response to terrorism must, however, go beyond condemnation and investigate the roots of such destructive behaviour. Furthermore the fight against terrorism 'presupposes the moral duty to help create those conditions that will prevent it from arising' (513). Since it is self-evident that 'the recruitment of terrorists is easier in situations where rights are trampled and injustices tolerated' (514) there must be a commitment to the creation of societies where the human rights of all are acknowledged and respected.

Though every society possesses a right to defend itself from terrorism this right has legal and moral limits. The response of the State must be carried out 'with respect for human rights and the principles of a State ruled by law' (514).

The Christian understanding of God leads it to judge as 'a profanation and a blasphemy' the notion of acting as a 'terrorist in God's name' (515). In the Christian tradition martyrdom cannot be the act of a person who kills in the name of God. Religions who claim to worship God cannot promote or condone terrorism but must work together to promote peace and solidarity among peoples and cultures.

Mt 5:9

Blessed are the peacemakers ...

The promotion of peace is an integral part of the Church's mission and finds concrete expression in its everyday work and prayer. The World Days of Peace, instituted by Pope Paul VI, provide the Church and people of goodwill with a concrete opportunity to commit themselves afresh to working for peace.

Pointers for further discussion

1 'Peace is not merely the absence of war, nor can it be reduced solely to the maintenance of a balance of power between enemies. Rather it is founded on a correct understanding of the human person and requires the establishment of an order based on justice and charity.' (494)

- Why is peace from the Christian perspective not just the 'maintenance of a balance of power'? Can you name places in our world where peace is maintained in this way?

- Who is responsible for the promotion of peace in our society and world?

- How essential are global justice and development for the establishment of peace?

- What actions could you take at a local level to contribute to the establishment of global peace?

2 'The damage caused by an armed conflict is not only material but also moral. In the end, war is "the failure of all true humanism", "it is always a defeat for humanity": "never again some

people against others, never again! ... No more war, no more war!"' (497)

- Can you identify wars which have been called 'just wars'? Do you agree that they were indeed 'just'?

- In a world with weapons of mass destruction can war be defended morally?

- Has the 'just war', even in self-defence, credibility today?

- Is pacifism a credible option for individuals or states?

3 'The arms race does not ensure peace. Far from eliminating the causes of war, it risks aggravating them. Policies of nuclear deterrence, typical of the Cold War period, must be replaced with concrete measures of disarmament based on dialogue and multilateral negotiations.' (508)

- What do you know about disarmament and the debate about it over the years?

- Do you think there has been an advance on the question of disarmament over the past decade?

- Does the stockpiling of arms contribute to global injustice and underdevelopment?

- What positive actions can a parish or local group take to counteract an arms race culture?

PART 5

The Church's Social Doctrine and Irish Society

Chapter Eight

The Irish context

Challenges and opportunities

Over the decades the Irish Catholic Bishops' Conference have applied the content and spirit of Catholic social teaching to Irish society and to the international community.[1] In these pastoral letters they have teased out the implications of Catholic teaching in the areas of the economy, politics and international relationships. They identified areas within Irish society that needed to be transformed in light of the Church's social principles.

A recent pastoral letter that focused on Irish society, *Prosperity with a Purpose,* deserves attention because it identifies the opportunities and challenges created by the Celtic Tiger. These include the creation of a society in Ireland that is inclusive, just and attentive to the rights of the global community; that has the ability to live in a way that makes real the virtue of solidarity.

The final part of the *Companion* will examine this pastoral letter and highlight its central insights and challenges. I will refer to the text itself, as before, by indicating the relevant paragraph in closed brackets.

Part 3 of the pastoral letter looks critically on the impact of the Celtic Tiger on the ethos of Irish society. Though it acknowledges the immense benefits that have resulted from Ireland's changed economic

---

1   Irish Catholic Bishops' Conference, *The Work of Justice,* Veritas, 1977; *Work is the Key,* Veritas, 1992; *Prosperity with a Purpose,* Veritas, 1999; *Towards the Global Economy,* Veritas, 2005.

fortunes it identifies several features of Irish society that need to be addressed.

The common good

From the outset the Bishops advance the common good as the rightful goal of economic activity. They embrace the definition of the common good found in Vatican II and make it their own: 'the sum total of all those conditions of social life which enable individuals, families and organisations to achieve complete and effective fulfilment' (40).

The Bishops argue that the common good is not automatically served by market forces (41). The market needs to be tempered and guided by the principles of justice, solidarity and inclusion. They argue that the Celtic Tiger 'requires the exercise of greater solidarity then ever by Irish men and women' (42). Though the economic boom has made inroads into poverty there is real evidence of a 'growth in serious income inequalities' in Irish society (56). This gives rise to two parallel worlds with very different expectations, experiences and opportunities. From the perspective of the Church's social doctrine this is a disturbing trend which needs to be reversed if the common good is to be promoted.

They identify the expensive housing market and the persistent reality of homelessness as 'perhaps the most evident example of a conflict between market forces and the common good' (43). In the midst of the economic boom house prices have risen to such an extent that a growing number of people cannot afford to buy houses. This situation works against the common good of Irish society because it denies to many an experience that contributes to personal and family well-being

The environment

Stewardship of the environment (49–52) is also a significant moral issue in a vibrant and expanding economy. The opportunity to raise the standard of living of the current generation must not be achieved 'at the expense of the quality of air and water, landscapes and general experience of nature' available to the next generation (50). There is a responsibility on public authorities (51) and on each person (52) to ensure that the environment is handed on to future generations 'ennobled and not disfigured'. Christians, in particular, are reminded to act in ways that acknowledge that the earth has its own 'requisites and a prior God-given purpose' (52).

Education

Another challenge of the Celtic Tiger identified by the Catholic Bishops is the reality of early school leavers (67–9). A booming economy provides an incentive to young people to leave school early and enter the world of work. This trend, while bringing short-term gains, does make people vulnerable to future long-term unemployment. If the economy was to change for the worst those without a proper education and skills could face a bleak future.

Poverty blackspots

There is also evidence in the 'new' Ireland of increasing urban 'poverty blackspots' that lead to marginalisation and anti-social behaviour (70–7). Rural disadvantage (78–83) and poverty is also evident. Both of these realities need to be addressed if the economic boom is to serve the needs of all. The increase in the quality of life of the many cannot be achieved or sustained at the expense of a marginalised and vulnerable minority.

Inclusion

A vibrant economy such as Ireland needs to be inclusive of peoples and groups who have often been neglected. People with disabilities (84–6) need to be included and provided for more adequately. Pope John Paul II has challenged us on this question: 'it would be a denial of our common humanity to admit to the life of the community, and thus to work, only those who are fully functional' (86). A more inclusive and caring society would also have to look at the reality of the Irish prison population (87–9). For many the experience of prison only serves to further alienate them from society and facilitates further anti-social behaviour. By international standards the Irish prison population is very young and 'recidivism is remarkably high' (88). The common good of Irish society demands that we examine both the treatment of prisoners and the realities that contribute to a culture of anti-social behaviour.

The Irish Bishops identify two other groups that need to be included and provided for in the booming Irish economy. The first group is the Travelling people (91–4) whose situation has become more difficult in the current economic boom. In a previous pastoral letter the Irish Bishops confronted the reality of prejudice, low life expectancy and poverty among the Travelling community.[2] Research indicates that progress in this area has been painfully slow and prejudice and marginalisation continue to be viscous realities in Irish life. This reality is in sharp contrast to the Gospel vision of solidarity that highlights our shared humanity.

---

2 *The Work of Justice*, par. 39.

Finally refugees and asylum seekers (95–7) provide Irish society with a new challenge and opportunity. There is some evidence that attitudes of intolerance and prejudice have found new targets in these vulnerable groups. The challenge for Irish society is to respond to them in ways that recognise and respect their humanity and integrate them into the mainstream of life. The Bishops are unequivocal in their judgement that 'harbouring racist thoughts and attitudes is a sign against the specific message of Christ' (96).

In Chapter 4 of the same publication the Bishops look at the underlying attitudes and values that inform many in Irish society as they enjoy the fruits of the Celtic Tiger. From the perspective of the Christian vision consumerism and materialism are very real threats to the well-being of the person because they encourage us to see the person as one-dimensional.

Lk 12:15

Inward looking?

At the beginning of their reflections the Irish Bishops remind us that 'economic over-development and moral underdevelopment are frequently found together' (99). Societies that experience significant levels of material well-being are often societies that lose their sense of human solidarity and of justice. They can become preoccupied with their own comfort and grow indifferent to the plight of others, especially the poor and vulnerable. At this level the challenges facing Irish society are significant. Are we in danger of becoming a society that is insular, individualistic and lacking in the virtue of human solidarity?

... a man's life is not made secure by what he owns, even when he has more than he needs.

More of everything but time?

In their musings on the 'quality' of Irish society the Bishops raise some very significant questions that deserve further reflection. They claim that in the booming economy we have more of everything but time; more money, cars, holidays but less time to spend with one another (101–11). The economic boom creates pressures that limit the amount of time we have for our families and loved ones. The Bishops also point out that, ironically, in the booming economy we have less security than we had (112–18). Constant change is a feature of the present economy and this generates its own pressures and insecurities. People are expected to be ever flexible, available and mobile in their work. This can impact negatively on the person and family. Given this reality they ask whether such a situation really contributes to our well-being as individuals and as a community. Though our 'quality of life', from the perspective of material comfort, may be improving, the 'human' quality of our lives and relationships is diminishing. This raises a significant question about our priorities as individuals and as a society: should the quality of our relationships be more important than material comfort?

Children

The rearing of children also involves new responsibilities and challenges in a booming economy. In the current economic climate children are a key consumer market (119–21) that is aggressively targeted by companies. The power of the designer label is very great among children and adults. This situation creates a new challenge for parents: to impress on their children that human happiness is not to be found in material goods. What is important is 'who we are' as persons rather than 'what we have'. As a practical response to this challenge the Bishops suggest that Ireland should follow the example of some other nations and place limits on the scope of advertising directed at children.

In conclusion the Bishops suggest that even though wealth can generate in us attitudes that are less than wholesome it can also be the opportunity for great acts of solidarity and sharing. It 'constitutes a mountain of opportunities' (123) that if grasped could contribute to a more inclusive and altruistic society in Ireland.

What kind of future?

Having examined in a critical way the reality of Irish life in the era of the Celtic Tiger the Bishops, in Chapter 5, focus their attention on the future. What are the great challenges and opportunities that confront Irish society with its new-found wealth? What are the key insights from the Church's social doctrine that need to be brought to life and embedded in concrete actions and structures?

In the vision of the Irish Bishops there is a need for the 'further development of Ireland's solidarity with the poorest nations and in the forging of a stronger ethic of consumption, of work and of civic responsibility within Ireland' (126). The challenge for Ireland is to continue with strong economic growth that is 'compatible with compassion, inclusiveness, global solidarity and environmental responsibility' (132).

Mt 5:6

Happy those who hunger and thirst for what is right: they shall be satisfied.

Solidarity with poorer nations

A primary challenge for Irish society is to look beyond itself and share its prosperity with poorer nations (127–32). The Bishops emphatically state that we must grasp this 'opportunity to make solidarity with poorer nations an even stronger dimension of Irish life' (129). The principle of the universal destination of the world's resources must find concrete expression in a time of unprecedented wealth in Ireland. It is also necessary in this time of plenty to develop 'a more mature relationship with the EU, viewing it no longer mainly as a source of support for Irish economic development' (131) but rather as an institution with the power to create a more just world economic order. Ireland must grasp the opportunity to play a robust role in encouraging the EU to develop relationships with the developing world that make solidarity, justice and inclusion more attainable.

The common good of Irish society

The challenges facing Irish society are also varied and complex. The fundamental question to be addressed is how the economy can be developed and directed to best serve the demands of the common good. The Bishops acknowledge that though Christians can validly differ as to which policies better serve the common good they 'will be united in urging a wider and deeper conversion to it in the first place' (133).

A consistent insight of the Church's social doctrine is that the dignity of the human person (136–8) is the foundation on which the common good is built. Consequently it is 'the criterion by which every political, economic and social development is to be judged' (136). All activity in the State is ultimately at the service 'of the whole person and of every person' (138).

Responsible consumers?

Great wealth is a relatively new experience in Ireland and raises important questions about our role as consumers. Are we responsible consumers? Do we look to our freedom and power as consumers for ultimate meaning and happiness? The pastoral letter argues that there is an urgent need to develop what it calls 'an ethic of consumption' (139–44). It readily acknowledges also that this is 'probably the least developed area of the Church's social teaching' (139). The essential foundation for the development of such an ethic depends on making a distinction between needs and wants, basics and luxuries. This distinction is becoming more blurred in Irish society. This can ultimately lead to an emphasis on 'having' rather than 'being'; measuring life and its meaning in terms of material possessions. A critical look at our role as consumers is needed in many areas of life – designer clothes, household luxuries, frequent holidays and the consumption of alcohol. It is ironic that in the past the abuse of alcohol was often linked to the depression and poverty of a society in economic stagnation (143). Today such abuse is often linked to the stress and pressures of economic success.

An ethic of work

If the Irish economy and society want to move forward in a way that benefits the common good of all it needs to develop a more consistent ethic of work (145–52). Such an ethic must have as its foundation a recognition of and respect for the subjective dimension of work. The dignity of work flows, not from the nature of the work being done or the amount of money being earned, but from the fact that it is a person who is doing the work. All work – paid, unpaid, skilled and unskilled – has a dignity because of this subjective dimension. A wholesome ethic of work would also ensure that work is structured in such a way that it enables and supports family life (151). This should include the provision of part-time employment and adequate benefits for childcare. Such an ethic would also embrace the special requirements of the low-skilled and immigrants. In the case of the latter the pastoral reminds us of the biblical injunction: 'be mindful of the stranger in your midst! You were a stranger once, in the land of Egypt' (Lev 19:34).

A robust and renewed ethic of work would also have implications for the public sector (159–62). A culture or ethos that links the value of work to the amount earned has the potential to destroy the traditional ethos of the public sector that emphasised service to the common good. The language of vocation is very much part of this traditional ethos. A renewed ethic of work would emphasise that it is the subjective dimension of work and its service to people that gives each job its true value. Payment 'acknowledges rather than confers' this value (162).

The pastoral letter acknowledges the right to strike (161) under strict conditions: is there a real injustice present? Is this injustice grave enough to justify the loss and damage likely to be caused? Is there a proper proportion between the loss about to be inflicted and the lawful end pursued? Have all efforts been made to reach settlement by negotiation, and have these efforts failed? The moral justification for strike action requires a clear 'Yes' to each of these four questions.

Finally the pastoral notes the need for an ethic of civic responsibility (163–73) that would promote and enshrine the values of transparency, honesty, fairness, accountability and respect for the common good (165). Voting responsibly and active participation in unions and voluntary organisations help serve and promote such an ethic (172).

The challenges and opportunities facing an economically vibrant Irish society are very great. It has the opportunity to become a more inclusive, just and environmentally responsible society. To achieve this end it must develop an ethic of work and of consumption that places the integral development of the person at its centre. In terms of its relationship with other peoples and nations Irish society is challenged to embrace, with even greater energy and commitment, the virtue of solidarity that recognises the oneness of the human family and the universal destiny of the earth's resources.

Pointers for further discussion

1 'One thing that rapid economic growth undoubtedly appears to do is make time a scarce resource.' (102)

- Discuss this idea and explore how it might be true in your own life and family.

- What are the implications of this development for the lives of couples, children and the elderly? Are there people in our society who have plenty of time? Why are they not affected by these changes?

- In a booming economy what decisions or choices can we make in order to 'find time'?

2 'There are some worrying signs that Ireland's civic culture may be weakening rather than strengthening. The percentage of the population exercising their right to vote in national elections has been steadily declining .... Voluntary organisations of practically every sort are experiencing increasing difficulties in retaining and attracting volunteers.' (171)

- In your view is 'Ireland's civic culture' weakening? If so, what are the causes of this decline? On what do you base this view?

- Can you identify projects and programmes that are aimed at building up our civic culture?

- Are you participating in any such initiatives?

3 'Wealth is an enormous latent power for doing good in a world as needy as our own. Divine revelation helps us see that either wealth is shared, or its owners become the owned and are diminished in themselves.' (173)

- How are we living with our new-found wealth in Ireland today?

- Are there positive aspects to our use of money that are not in the public eye nor reported in the media?

- What are the challenges and opportunities that come with Ireland's new-found wealth? How can you and your parish/community respond to these?

General Index